THE CARPENTER
AND HIS KINGDOM

by

ALEXANDER IRVINE

AUTHOR OF "*My Lady of the Chimney Corner,*"
"*The Souls of Poor Folks,*" etc.

NEW YORK
CHARLES SCRIBNER'S SONS
1922

CONTENTS

CHAPTER I

THE FRIEND WHO PREPARED THE WAY

CHAPTER II

IN THE DAYS OF HIS YOUTH

CHAPTER III

BEGINNING AT CAPERNAUM

CONTENTS

CHAPTER IV

VOICES HE HEARD IN THE WOODS

CHAPTER V

THE CIRCLE OF INTIMATE FRIENDS

CHAPTER VI

THE MIND OF THE MASTER

CHAPTER VII

THE MASTER AND LABOUR

CONTENTS

CHAPTER VIII

HIS MIND AND OTHER MINDS

CHAPTER IX

THE MASTER'S MAGNA CHARTA

CHAPTER X

THE KINGDOM OF GOD

CONTENTS

CHAPTER XI

THE KINGDOM IN ACTION

CHAPTER XII

THE EMOTIONS OF JESUS

CHAPTER XIII

THE HUMANITY OF THE MASTER

CHAPTER XIV

MISSING THE MARK

CONTENTS

CHAPTER XV

THE MASTER AND MAMMON

CHAPTER XVI

CONSPIRACY AND MURDER

CHAPTER XVII

WHO THEN ARE CITIZENS OF THE KINGDOM?

THE CARPENTER AND HIS KINGDOM

CHAPTER I

THE FRIEND WHO PREPARED THE WAY

¶ I

The Records

THE story of John the Baptist as found in the Gospels is amazingly brief. Mark tells it in a few sentences. Matthew gives more than twice as much material as Mark, but half of it concerns the miraculous incidents surrounding John's birth. Luke gives the longest account, but two-thirds of it concern the life of John's father and mother.

The account in the fourth Gospel is brief but dramatic. In the first three Gospels, John is objective, intense—a man of action. In the fourth he is subjective, and is used as a reflector of the light of the Logos.

All of them write of John with a distinctly theological motive. One dominant note pervades them all. John was the fulfilment of the Old Testament prophecy. He is made to fit with accuracy into frames made by Elijah and Isaiah and Malachi. That, however, does not rob him of personality. In the Gospels there is one major and many minor characters. John is the major of all minors.

Fragments of Information

At least a generation passed before any one committed to writing the events which convulsed Israel in John's day. That is a long time to trust even the best memories. What we get in the Gospels is not a biography. We get a synopsis of the life of Jesus and fragments of information concerning the life of John. The essentials are there. Sometimes, they are in the form of unattractive naked truth, sometimes in truth that is clothed and articulate, which is a higher form of the same thing.

Pen Picture of John

The picture of John is that of an unkempt and uncouth man who suddenly bursts upon the scene and with a fiery tongue calls upon the people to repent. The response is immediate and sincere. There must have been those who knew him. He was born at Hebron of well-known parents. He belonged to the order of the priesthood, but from the beginning he stood outside the pale of either synagogue or temple. The time was ripe for change. Religion had degenerated into dead formalism. The new voice seemed full of hope. He had just emerged from the Wilderness, where for years he had been concentrating his mind on spiritual things. Israel was in dire need of a revival, and the revivalist had arrived. Instantly there followed what seemed a massed conviction of sin, and the people in large crowds followed him wherever he went. He was a rather violent contrast to the special caste of religious goodness known as the Pharisees. He was without official sanction, he belonged to none of the prevalent schools. Ruthlessly he had thrown aside their time-honoured customs of feasts, fast, and phalacteries. His shaggy black hair was matted on his white brow. Instead of a priestly jibba, he wore the untanned skin of a wild beast, which was held close to his body by a rough leather thong. He not only threw overboard the useless baggage of prescribed habiliments, but he discarded the law as it related to food. He lived on what nature provided in the fastnesses of the mountains, the honey of wild bees and locusts and dried flies. He avoided all kinds of strong drink, he ate no flesh. In the storehouse of nature everything to him was Kosher. It is more than probable that John had spent some years with the Essenes, a Jewish sect that was a protest against Judaism. It was a communistic cult that lived the simple life in the wilderness where they worshipped God, cultivated the soil, and held things in common.

¶ 2

Essenism and Christianity

Christian historians have always seemed very much afraid to say anything commendable about the apparent strivings of this off-shoot of Judaism, which was more in common with Christianity than with the religion of Israel. That it was an ethical and spiritual improvement on the older system, none can deny. They prohibited oaths, they prohibited slavery, they healed the sick, and devoted themselves to fasting and prayer. With regard to slavery they did not content themselves with holding a theory about it. They forbade its practice absolutely within their jurisdiction. In comparing the Christian and Essenic attitude toward slavery, Neander says: 'The law of the Essenes prohibited and so was Christ's intended to subvert it The sect agreed with the Saviour in seeing that all men alike bear the image of God, and that none have the right by holding their fellows as property, to degrade that image into a brute or a chattel So far, Essenism and Christianity agree, but see wherein they differ. The one was a formula for *a small circle* of devotees; the other was a system for the regeneration of mankind: the one made positive enactments, acting by pressure from without, the other implanted new moral principles to work from within: the one put its law in force at, and declared that no slave could be held in the communion: the other gave no direct command upon the subject. Yet the whole spirit of Christ's teaching tended to create in men's minds a moral sense of the evil of a relation so utterly subversive of all that is good in humanity, and thus to effect its entire prohibition.'

The soundness of a principle does not depend upon the number of people who hold it—even though a great German historian says it does. The simple answer to Neander's comparison is, that despite what Christ's teaching 'tended to create' in men's mind, it did not create it sufficiently effectively to abolish slavery. Christians practised and believed in it for over eighteen centuries after Christ's death.

Foolish Fear

The background of such casuistry seems to be a hidden fear that the Essenes exerted an influence on the beginnings of Christianity. The fear, though foolish, is well founded. Like the Pilgrim Fathers, the Essenes went out and braved the dangers and desolations of the deserts in order to be free to worship God according to the new light. The sect did not take the world by storm. Pioneers blaze a pathway and lay foundations, others follow and build. The Essenes followed their light, but their light faded, as the rays of a candle fade before the brighter rays of the sun.

A Candle in Sunlight

If John the Baptist came out from amongst them it was because his dominating personality was too pronounced to fuse in the democratic community. He followed their glimmer until he saw the brighter light. As they outgrew Judaism, he outgrew them. The red-hot message of his fiery soul demanded a larger anvil on which to be hammered out. On the banks of the Jordan he found a world anvil in the workshop of the world's religion.

¶ 3

The Ministry of the Baptist

Let us examine his message: It was a trumpet call
to repentance. The call was not new. He gave it a
new emphasis. When the Rabbis called, Israel seemed
deaf. The prophets had called, but they were all dead;
their call had been committed to writing, but it was
a mere echo—revered but disregarded. The call of
Isaiah was the most pungent, the most clear. It was
a diagnosis, a rebuke, and a remedy. He saw the
decay of the spirit and the growth of formalism. He
told Israel it was futile to afflict their souls and leave
the state of the soul unchanged. He told them that
God could make Jews out of the stones under their feet.

What to do

A crowd on the banks of Jordan differed little from
a crowd on the banks of the Thames or the Rhine or
the Hudson. 'What shall we do?' they shouted at
John. They know just as well as John, how to realise
the ideal presented, but they wanted the assistance of
his authority and the moral pressure of his advice.
To readjust themselves mentally, was an easy task,
but the adoption of a new mental attitude, that would
disturb their economic status was not quite so easy.
His answers were apt and to the point. They were to
get out of the darkness and to face the light. They
were to throw off heavy burdens that shackled their
souls, and in spiritual freedom bring forth works meet
for repentance, and in harmony with their changed
condition of mind. The background of John's power
was not merely the spiritual passion that possessed
him. He was the exemplification of what he taught.
His programme was less revolutionary than that of
Jesus, but as far as it went it was just as specific.
Micah, in what is considered the highest ethical note
in the Old Testament, tells Israel that the supreme

requirements of Jehovah are: 'to do justly, to love mercy, and to work humbly with God.'

The Mass Mind

On the banks of the Jordan, John reiterates with power this message. His words burned themselves into the conscience. Under such burning eloquence the crowd acts as one person, it moves in a positive direction. A reaction may come later—when the barrage lifts, they think. But for the time being, the crowd is moved out of a negative into a positive state of mind. It was thus with John's preaching. The Evangelists tell us that all Judea and all Jerusalem came out to hear and were baptized. All may have gone out, and all may have undoubtedly been influenced, but when John castigated without reserve certain groups and called them 'a generation of vipers,' we must understand that a reaction followed, and he was as bitterly opposed by those in power as was Jesus.

Answers to Questions

Luke groups the questioners. To a certain group— evidently the well-to-do—John said: 'he that hath two coats let him impart to him that hath none, and he that hath meat, let him do likewise.' Then came the Publicans, and to their questions he answered: 'extort no more than that which is appointed you.' The soldiers came and put the same questions, and he said: 'Put not man in fear, accuse no man falsely and be content with your allowance.'

Living Word

One Evangelist tells us that he characterised the multitude as a generation of vipers, and another says he reserved that characterisation for the Pharisees and Sadducees. The latter may have had it twice without feeling that they had more than their share. The more intelligent of those who listened must have recognised the words of Malachi in his discourses, but it would be a mistake to suppose that it was a mere mechanical reiteration. His work lay athwart the lines of priestly routine, but his words they had considered dead. The same is true of his baptism. He gave a new meaning to an old institution. Baptism was not an exclusively Jewish rite. The surrounding nations had practised it in a variety of forms.

¶ 4

The Meeting of Jesus and John

The introduction of Jesus and John is sudden and dramatic. Although cousins, they were apparently strangers to each other. They followed widely divergent pathways—pathways which however widely apart now merged in an angle for a moment before diverging again. Scientific men have utterly failed to locate the spot where the meeting occurred. It is just as well. It was the locality of the spirit from which a new way led out—away out—to the ends of the earth.

'And it came to pass in those days that Jesus came from Nazareth and was baptized of John in the Jordan.'

Thus Mark condenses in one brief sentence material enough for many volumes. Matthew adds a significant detail. When Jesus asked for Baptism, John demurred: 'I have need to be baptized of thee, and comest Thou to me?' This may imply either previous acquaintance or a knowledge gained at the moment by the keen penetrating intellect of the Baptist. The latter seems the most probable though both may be true. **'Suffer it to be so *now*,'** Jesus said, **'for thus it becometh us to fulfil all righteousness.'**

We are not quite clear as to the meaning of this sentence, but the fact that He was baptized in the Jordan by John and in the presence of a multitude is sufficient to convince us that He considered it the correct thing to do.

¶ 5

Baptism

Baptism is a symbol, an outward symbol of an inward spiritual fact. It is more than that, it is a symbol of unity—unity of faith and purpose. It is also the gateway into the Kingdom. In the ministry of John it followed confession of sin. It typified the cleansing of the soul. Jesus accepted it not for His own sake, but as an act of leadership and in endorsement of John and as an example to the flock, out of which He was to draw His disciples later.

In the passing centuries, Baptism has changed not only in form but in substance. With some it remains what it was on the banks of the Jordan—the symbol of a new life. With others it became a sacrament, and as such, to them, an essential in the plan of salvation. This conception has been carried to such an extreme that the door of the kingdom of heaven swings on the hinges of this strange theory.

Conflicting Theories

Ecclesiastical rigour has somewhat relaxed. Until recently the damnation of infants was an accepted tenet of some creeds. Even baptized infants had to receive the Eucharist or be equally damned with the unbaptized. This was harder on the Ecclesiastics than on the infants—whom it affected only in theory. That such theories should be based on the Gospel, and that they should have persisted so long, seems incomprehensible. In our day there is more liberty of interpretation. The controversy over baptism, though not yet relegated to the limbo of extinct controversies has been considerably modified. There are many forms, but there is one baptism. There is but one Kingdom, but there are many entrances. The letter mystifies before it kills—it is the spirit of the thing that illuminates and gives life.

¶ 6

Differences

At all points of personal contact Jesus and John
are in perfect harmony.   John came first and prepared
the way.   When Jesus came He at once recognised
and proclaimed him.   From the first moment there is
no variableness nor shadow of turning in the Baptist.
Why the two leaders should go different ways we do
not know.   John goes his way and his disciples follow
him.   Jesus was as yet without followers.   He goes and
calls disciples.   He never repudiated John.   John was
true to death.

Misunderstanding

In the course of time there arose misunderstandings
between the two groups of disciples.   John had a strict
training.   Naturally he imparted part of the discipline
to his followers.   When Jesus had called His disciples
and had entered upon His ministry, His disciples said:
'Master, teach us to pray, as John also taught his
disciples.'   The answer of Jesus was the Lord's Prayer.
When the disciples of John heard of the popularity of
Jesus they spoke to John about it.   John's reply is
characteristic: 'He that hath the bride is the bridegroom: but the friend of bridegroom, which standeth
and heareth him rejoiceth at the bridegroom's voice:
this my joy therefore is fulfilled.'
Later the disciples of John came to Jesus and said:
'Why do we and the Pharisees fast, and Thy disciples
fast not?'   It is a simple question simply put.   It
shows they were on friendly terms and familiar.
The answer of Jesus is startling.   He takes the
very metaphor John used, and by it illustrates
His answer: **'Can the sons of the bridechamber
mourn as long as the bridegroom is with them?
But the days shall come when the bridegroom shall
be taken away from them—then shall they fast.'**

The Winnowing Fan

Here were differences, but they were differences of
feethod. The two groups were travelling along dif-
mrent roads, but they were journeying toward the same
destination. John went on preaching and baptizing.
His enthusiasm did not wane. The urge of the soul
drove him into an unusual self-abandonment. He spoke
without caution or reserve. His words were like barbed
arrows. Where they penetrated they remained. Crowds
continued to listen and followers increased, but the
officials began to oppose him. His logic forced them to
seek cover in one of two positions. They must abandon
the old régime and follow him, or reject him and defend
it. They drew away from John. Soon he felt their
opposition. He had attacked sin in high places, that
relieved the Pharisees of personally bringing John to
task. They informed the court that he was dangerous.
He was. All men who have a sense of the reality of
God know not what fear is. They couldn't starve John.
They couldn't curtail his clothing. They could take
his life, but on that John himself set little value.

¶ 7

John Leaves Galilee

The leaven of the Pharisees began to work. The
huge gatherings dwindled down to negligible numbers,
and it was probably John's most intimate disciples who
urged him to continue his work, beyond the Jordan.
Details of his movements are very meagre. A sentence covers miles of travelling and months of time.
The scraps of information are used largely as filling
for the Evangelists in their difficult task of putting
together what men remembered. We do not know who
went with him. Disciples visited him in prison. They
probably went with him, and shared the pleasures and
hardships of the journey.

Truth and Simplicity

We do not read of him visiting his birthplace, nor do we know whether any of his relatives were amongst his followers. Home to him was where he found a couch. He carried no baggage. He had no encumbrances. For companions he had converts. His temple floor was the earth beneath his feet, the dome was the vault of heaven above his head. Instead of preistly robes of the temple service, be wore what nature provided in its rough, raw state. His food was simple and easily obtained. The requirements of the flesh were reduced to the lowest degree. He lived the simple life, millenniums before the world ever dreamed of a cult of that character. Life to him was a spiritual pilgrimage. The vision never grew dim. His mission changed not, whether he preached to crowds or small groups.

Somewhere out there beyond Jordan, he came in contact with Jesus for the last time. Some commentators are of the opinion that a change came over John. John 3, 31–36 is cited as evidence. The passage is in the language of the author. It is his style, his thought. It is mystical and theological. It looks like a running comment on the well-known humility and loyalty of the Baptist.

Taking into consideration the difference in the accounts, we have reason to believe that his ministry beyond Jordan was of brief duration. He had left the jurisdiction of Pilate, for the more dangerous territory of Herod Antipas.

Mark gives the fullest and most graphic account of John's arrest, and imprisonment by Antipas, though it is at this time that Luke and Matthew give us the most startling comment that Jesus ever made on John.

¶ 8

John in Prison

'Herodias had a quarrel with him and would have killed him,' says Mark 6, 19. John's fame had probably

preceded him.   His name was a household word in all
Judea and the surrounding countries.   The truth he
preached had a general application to all life, but there
evidently were times when he was tremendously specific.

John Attacks Sin in High Places

Herod Antipas and Herodias were married under
circumstances which outraged the moral sentiment of
the people over whom they vulgarly reigned.   In order
to effect the union Antipas divorced his wife, and Herodias discarded her husband, who was her own uncle and
brother to Antipas.   John probably not only told his
hearers, but Antipas himself to his face, what he thought
of the marriage.   Herodias made up her mind to put
John out of the way at once.   Antipas restrained her.
He feared the people.

The summary disposal of the revolutionist might precipitate the revolution, and the hands of the king were
already full.   Herod Antipas seems to have divided his
royal time between Tiberius and the fortress or castles
of Macherus in which John was imprisoned.   His followers had access to him.   Naturally his disciples were
depressed—and questioned John about the outcome of
his ministry, his imprisonment, the future, and, of
course, about his beloved Messiah.   Whatever John
said, whatever hope he gave them, the fact remained
that he was himself in the hand of Herod Antipas and
a prisoner!   One day when they were more discouraged
than usual, and consequently more clamorous in their
questions, John conceived an idea.   He knew that he
was the bond that held them together.   His dissolution
meant their disintegration.   The Messiah was in the
ascendancy.   John was withdrawing within the veil.
He had a duty to them as long as life lasted.   It was
to strengthen their faith, to lead them in their way.
We can easily imagine the rugged champion saying to
them: 'True, I am in irons and a victim of that king
of Bashan above, true, I am physically helpless to
break the power that holds me here, and in my helpless-

ness you ask me if I have changed my mind, on the
vision that came to me on the banks of the Jordan?
Go find the beloved One! Tell Him that he who lingers
in this dungeon cell, hath sent thee unto Him, saying:
'Art Thou that One? or shall we look for another?'
He will tell thee. He will show thee signs. He will
take the doubts from thy mind and the sorrow from
thine hearts. Then shall I die in peace.'

The men went off with their doubts As they went
they discussed the serious situation. The fate of John
looked hopeless. It was unlikely that Herod and Herodias would condone an attack that held them up to
the scorn of the people, by whose blood and sweat they
were enabled to live a voluptuous life. If John should
be put to death, and Jesus should not be the fulfilment
of their hope, the case was still worse—it was the death
of hope. From the darkness behind, to the light beyond, they travelled, and as they journeyed their hearts
burned within them with hope and fear.

The khans on the trade routes were the news centres
of those days. Travellers from all directions exchanged
the news of one part for that of another. By the inn-
keepers, the doubting disciples were directed to the
encampment of the Master and His disciples.

When they found Him they put the question: 'John
the Baptist hath sent us unto Thee saying: "Art Thou
He that should come, or wait we for another?"'

¶ 9

Jesus Sends an Answer to John

Jesus did not answer the question at once. He bade
them tarry, and while they tarried they watched.
He was fully conscious of the delicacy of the situation.
His Friend and Forerunner was entering the valley of
the shadow of death. It is possible that John was in
as much need of strength as were his followers. Great
men have their moods, their mountains, and valleys

of emotions, of faith, and of courage.   The answer to
the question must be specific and satisfactory.   It
was to be his last message to John.   The occasion
demanded—not a mere verbal reiteration, of what had
been heard before, but a demonstration.   While John's
followers waited they saw Him at work.   He was
surrounded as usual by the poor, the sick, the seekers
after truth, the sorrowing, and sin stricken.   His
ministry to their needs was His answer.   In substance He said to the followers of John: **'Go and tell
John that I am taking away the sin of the world,
I am healing the sick, giving sight to the blind,
loosing the slaves, and preaching the Gospel to the
poor.'**   It was His programme—the programme He
had preached in the Synagogue at Nazareth.

¶ 10

The Paradox

When John's disciples had left, Jesus turned to the
crowd around Him, and made a statement, the last
sentence of which is both startling and mysterious.
He said:—

**'What went ye out into the wilderness for to
see?   A reed shaken with the wind?   But what
went ye out for to see?   A man clothed in fine
raiment?   Behold they which are gorgeously ap-
parelled, and live delicately, are in King's courts.
But what went ye out for to see?**

**A Prophet?   Yea, I say unto you and more than
a Prophet.   This is he of whom it is written—
Behold I send my messenger before thy face,
which shall prepare thy ways before thee.   Verily
I say unto you that among them that are born
of woman, there hath not risen a greater than
John the Baptist: But he that is least in the
Kingdom of God is greater than he.'**

Luke vii. 24–28.

The account in Matthew is quite different, but the startling phrase is the same in both Gospels. Some commentators have ventured to suggest that when Jesus used the 'less than the least' phrase He referred to Himself. That is altogether improbable. On the other hand it seems still more improbable that He made it sum up the life and ministry of John.

Most of the commentators get over the difficulty by relegating John to the Old Testament dispensation. They do that by the same mental process that an ancient commentator explained the necessity for four Gospels—*i.e.*, 'because the earth has four corners!'

It may be that John was not the material out of which Jesus could make an ambassador. He probably was too much wedded to the old to engross Himself absolutely and wholly in the new. He was probably athwart the lines of the new progress, but we are not to suppose that Jehovah limited him to the system whose doom He had sent Him to pronounce. It is out of keeping with the scheme of things that Samson-like he should have taken hold of the pillars of the old regime, and brought it down on his own head with a crash. If the report is correct, Jesus did not deliver the pronunciamento until John's disciples had gone to Macherus. John therefore died in ignorance of his status.

The Editorial Hand

Neither Matthew nor Luke make any attempt to explain. There are many places in the New Testament where the editorial hand becomes apparent in offsetting possible erroneous impressions, and in correcting mistakes. The author of the fourth Gospel for instance tells us in one chapter that Jesus was baptizing and in the next corrects his mistake, and just as emphatically tells us that He baptized not. Peter tells us that there are many things in the epistles of his 'beloved brother Paul,' which are 'hard to understand.' John tells us that when Jesus spoke of His flesh as spiritual food, the disciples frankly confessed that they did not understand Him. We can only weigh one statement with another and arrive at a conclusion by an analysis of the spirit rather than the letter.

His Estimate of John

The statement of Jesus concerning John is inexplicable because it is out of harmony with the invariable and consistent attitude He bore to His messenger. **'He was a burning and a shining light,'** said Jesus in speaking of him, and whatever the meaning of the other phrase may be, we are justified in believing that the light was bright enough to illuminate his pathway out of the old theocracy into the new Kingdom.

¶ II

A Bacchanalian Feast

Herod Antipas had several interviews with John. Despite John's plainness of speech, Herod considered him 'a good man and holy.' According to Luke, John was not merely concerned about Herod's domestic affairs, he was familiar with the vile record, and probably went over the itemised account in detail. Herod was amused, interested, and at times in terror. The interview reminds us strongly of another such, between Elijah and Ahab. In each case a prophet in rags stands before a King arrayed in purple and fine linen, moral majesty at both interviews confronting a crowned murderer.

Herod's birthday came. Great preparations had been made. From the Gospels we learn the kind of people who were invited The army leaders, the rich merchants, and the land owners, the court officials, and whatever or whoever of the parasitic retainers could be put under obligation for such an honour.

Wine, Women, and Music

It was a small Balshazar's feast with the usual oriental trimmings. It was a feast of wine, women, and music.

Herodias was the master mind of the occasion. She had prepared a subtle stroke for the Batpist. Salome, her daughter, was used as the medium by which she was to catch the king and hold him where he was weakest.

The daughter was young and beautiful. She had prepared her part, and acted it well. After the food and wine, the king and queen and their guests lounged around the hall, while Salome performed one of those pirouetting performances that never fail to make an appeal to the masculine mind. There are dances which are music in motion. They appeal to the æsthetic sense —the sense of the best and the beautiful in us. There are dances which light up into conflagration all the fires of our lower nature! Of Salome's contribution we need only point to the result. It was the subtlest kind of a voluptuous exhibition of writhing, suggestive, pirouetting beauty.

The Sensuous Scene

Herodias divided her attention between the lecherous glances of Herod and the twisting, half-naked form of her daughter. She was playing a dangerous game, but the stakes were high. She may have had fear but it was negligible compared with the spirit of revenge that filled her heart like a nest of scorpions. Herod was affected by the dance of his adopted daughter. The glare of the colours, the glamour of the music, the fascination of the form and motion were supplemental to the wine-warmed blood in his veins. In a two-fold sense he was intoxicated and loudly applauded the sensuous scene. Before the dancer could stretch herself on a divan he was at her feet: 'Ask of me what you will,' he said passionately, 'and I will give it thee, even to the half of my kingdom.'

Salome's Request

Salome consulted her mother, and immediately announced her choice. 'I will that thou give me forthwith in a charger the head of John the Baptist.'

'And the king was exceeding sorry,' we are told. The request staggered him. He knew not the heart of Herodias, nor was he aware of the part played by Salome. In the heart of the most insensate brute, there is a residue of what we call conscience. He knew it was morally wrong, and a political blunder, but he had promised, and the guests had heard him. He had refused Herodias, he knew that he ought to refuse her daughter, but he lacked moral courage and took the easiest way.

¶ 12

John Beheaded

If Herod in his momentary hesitation had taken a look into the future, he would perhaps have decided differently. The decision he rendered has handed his name to the world for all time as a synonym of lust and murder. Herodias and Salome are none the less culpable, but in the word of Herod Antipas resided the power, and he used it in defiance of his conscience, to pay the price of a moment's pleasure.

> 'Right for ever on the scaffold,
> Wrong for ever on the throne;
> Yet that scaffold rules the future,
> And behind the great unknown;
> Standeth God amid the shadows,
> Keeping watch above His own.'

A soldier was summoned. John was aroused from his meditations and beheaded in his cell. The head was put in a charger and conveyed to the banqueting hall. It was handed to Salome, and she handed it to her mother. Herod Antipas probably awoke when the transfer of the ghastly gift revealed the motive. If he did, he awoke too late. He had unwittingly set the crown of martyrdom on the head of John, but the act did not mitigate the foul stench with which he had asso-

ciated his own name.   The fiendish procedure was the
finishing touch to a bacchanalia, the infamy of which
will resound throughout the world, wherever right is
contrasted with wrong, tyranny with liberty, and the
canker of lust with the purity of the human heart.

Thus died the first of the Master's friends—a saint,
a prophet, a martyr, and one whose imperishable glory
is that it was he who inaugurated the stupendous
spiritual revolution in Israel, the chief result of which
was the bringing forth of the founder of the Christian
religion to whom he pointed and said, 'Behold the
Lamb of God!'

CHAPTER II

¶ 13

Childhood

THE childhood of Jesus is veiled in mystery. Nothing
is known of His youth. The earliest writers wrote
from memory—their own, or the memory of others.
In sifting the true from the less true, or false, much
material had to be put aside as unavailable for their
purpose. The rejected material persisted, however,
and later found a place as a literature by itself. The
evangelists had a twofold purpose in writing: to record
the truth and meet the thought of their time. Some
knowledge of the facts and forces operating at the
beginning of the Christian Era is essential to an understanding of the life of Jesus. Hence this rapid survey
of the days of His youth.

In the Temple

Only once between infancy and His first appearance
in public is the veil drawn aside. It is a simple story,
consistent and authentic. At the age of twelve we
find Him in the temple questioning the doctors. The
story is without embellishment. There is a self-
consciousness—perhaps self-assertiveness that for a
child of twelve seems rather startling. While Joseph
and Mary imagined He was following them, He was
following the bent of His mind, and it led Him to the
House of Prayer. There, to their astonishment, they
found Him in the midst of the Elders of Israel. In
answer to His mother's questioning, He said: **'Wist**

ye not that I am about my Father's business?'
The language is unusual, but neither impetuous nor
precocious.

Joseph and Mary were of the common people. That
is an outstanding fact in all records. Whether Joseph's
line led back to Adam, to whom it is popularly supposed
we can all be traced, or whether it led to the throne of
David, the fact remains that the main social stream had
left him high and dry on the banks of a small tributary
—he was a carpenter.

Working People

If any apology had to be made for that to the
ancients, none is necessary to us. Kings are not always
points of departure to be proud of. They are a luxury
people cannot always afford. Carpenters are a necessity. Much literary effort has been spent in explaining
what Canon Farrar calls the 'fallen fortunes' of Joseph
and Mary. If Joseph 'fell' it is just possible that he
fell upward out of the parasitic, into the socially useful
class. 'If a man shall not work, neither shall he eat,'
was the dictum of Paul, and centuries earlier Moses
recorded a divine command that 'man should eat bread
in the sweat of his face'—his own, not the face of
another.

¶ 14

Nazareth

Nazareth, where He was brought up, was a Galilean
town which seems to have been of less than average
moral repute. No special charge is made against it,
but it was a man of more than ordinary intelligence who
asked: 'Can any good thing come out of Nazareth?'

Reputation of Nazareth

It is not unlikely that its evil reputation was intimately connected with questions of property. Nazareth was a Roman province, a centre of population and a usurers' paradise. Taxation was a heavy burden. The land was fruitful and yielded abundantly, but the more abundant the production, the heavier the tax. The richer the people grew, the poorer they became. There was a head tax on both bond and free. Doors, windows, pillars, corn, wheat, oil, fruit, trees, animals —all, everything was taxed to the limit and beyond. There was an army of tax-gatherers. They let and sub-let, and farmed out the various sections of the country. The tax-gatherers were Roman knights and apostate Jews. They were the publicans, the capitalists of the Roman Empire. Modern 'cornering' in corn and wheat, had its origin in the dawn of history, and in the cradle of the world. 'I will tear down my barns and build greater,' was a stock exchange expression of a Galilean speculator.

The lords temporal must have lost mucn sleep in the effort to invent new schemes of taxation, and the lords spiritual in fruitless efforts to determine whether it was a violation of the law, to eat an egg laid on the Sabbath! The labourer was in the same category. He was part of a system out of which there was no escape, save through the gates of death.

¶ 15

The Poor

Where the tax-gatherers, usurers, and exploiters left off, the temple and the synagogue began—with an intricate system of tithes and offerings. True, the poor could offer a pigeon if that was all that had been left them, but even in the sale of pigeons, the priests had cornered the market, and fixed the price about half a guinea each. Thus trodden beneath the heel of oppression, the human worms turned. At first the turning was mild. They protested, then they petitioned, then when there was no hope of relief, they revolted.

Revolutions are respectable only in success. Revolutionsists, when they succeed, are heroes and patriots. When they fail, they become criminals. It was a great Jewish teacher who said money was the root of all evil, but a careful study of Jewish history leads us to the belief that whatever of a criminal class there was in Galilee, was composed very largely of those from whom the root had been entirely extracted.

The Economic Factor

To Jesus as a boy and youth, these matters were things of common knowledge. The economic factor was one of his teachers in the school of life, and His own teaching teems with reference to it. The question: 'What shall we eat and drink, and wherewithal shall we be clothed?' was fundamental. Before we can have moral life, we must have life. It was not the only fundamental question. There was a spiritual revolt against a religion that pressed down as heavily on the soul as robbery and exploitation bore down on the body.

Rabbinical punctiliousness had its origin in a patriotic and religious effort to stem the tide of foreign influence. The temple had been profaned. Augustus provided that sacrifices should be offered daily at his expense, to the most high God. It was a sop, of course, but there were those who looked upon it as a compliment.

Strange Gods

Despite all vigilance, heathen temples and heathen deities had invaded the land. Apollo, Jupiter, and Hercules were enshrined at Gaza, and shared the honours with Diana, Juno, and Venus.

Ascalon added Mercury, Castor and Pollux, Minerva and Astarte. In Caesarea Philippi, Herod built a temple for the worship of Augustus. Heathenism had its temples in every important place in Palestine. Herod opened the gates, and the gods trooped in, in scores. Jehovah seemed to be subordinated, and His religion

seemed to be losing its force, even for the house ot Israel.
Revolts over foreign taxation were followed by physical
resistance to foreign religion.   After each, there were
massacres, in which thousands were put to death.   When
pestilence and famine came, they were looked upon as
scourges of God, for the profanation of the temple, but
the Roman Eagles still flew overhead, and the taxes
were still collected.   Thus the tide of human life ebbed
and flowed.

¶ 16

Origin of Pharisaism

On the practical side, the organised expression was
the Zelots, on the religious side, the Pharisees.   For
the history and influence of these sects we must look,
not to the New Testament, but to Jewish history.
The Evangelists give us vivid pictures of the extreme
of these sects, as they come in contact with the Master,
but the fact that during His ministry He accepted
hospitality from Pharisees is proof enough that He saw
a side of the sect, not fully presented in the Gospels.

Sects

For over a hundred years B.C. the Pharisees had
been a school within a school, a sect within a sect, in
Judaism.   They stood next to the Rabbis as trustees
and defenders of the faith.   There was a laxity in the
observance of the law.   They were the yeast stirrers
among the delinquents.   There was a pressure of foreign
religious influence from without.   They fought it.   Zeal
needs organisations.   They organised.   Within organisation, there were steps of development, degrees of
sanctity.   They organised groups of brotherhoods to
cover the need.   These groups were all inclusive.   There
was no social caste, it was open to the people.   Whoever
desired to observe laws, in the spirit of the fathers, was
eligible and might take the vow.   There was a period

of probation and promotion according to progress.
There was no jealousy, the movement had the sanction
of the Rabbis and the co-operation of the people, the
priestly families who felt that their hereditary privileges
were in danger. The organised expression of the priestly
families was the Sadducees.

They were wealthy and had vested interests. They
were not sticklers for the law, yet strangely enough,
they were the high church party, and conservatives
in matters relating to the temple, the priesthood, and
official religion.

Beliefs

The Pharisees were the Liberals. They were for the
temple also but they were for the synagogue, the school,
and the teacher. They were propagandists for personal
religion. There was one cardinal difference. The
Sadducees believed that the soul died with the body.
The Pharisees believed in immortality. The Sadducees
were fatalistic. God had made man and handed over
to him the reins of his own destiny. This done, God
withdrew. Such a belief they found convenient. It
enabled them to enjoy life as they found it, without the
limitations that were so binding upon their compatriots.
The Pharisees kept alive the hope of a coming Kingdom
of Heaven ,but they also believed that it was to come
about by the co-operation of man with Jehovah.

Pharisaism

They believed in repentance and love to one's neighbour, and this not for the Jews alone, but for the Gentile
World. This comes nearer to the teaching of the Master,
than the Pharisees are popularly supposed to have come,
yet they were His bitterest opponents, and ultimately,
it was with their co-operation that He was put to death.

The second change in the life of the Pharisees, was
more subtle than the Sadducees. It was a spiritual

conceit, and exaggerated egotism that rendered their feasts a farce and their rites and ceremonies a dumb show. The change was gradual, but decay was sure. We are indebted, not to the records of Christianity for a full description of Pharisaism, but to the Mishna and other writings of Jews themselves. In these writings no phase of the surrounding heathenism was so thoroughly castigated as the final hypocrisy of the Pharisees.

¶ 17

A Ponderous Code of Laws

The last phase was a sort of ecclesiastical manicuring with the law. Pharisees and Rabbis spent their lives in the most trifling casuistry and inane puerilities, endless discussion, endless division of opinion as to what was clean and unclean in matters of food and furniture, work and workshops. There was a 'thus saith the Lord' for every act of life—for feasts and fasts, for tithes and offerings, for meats and drinks, for reading and conversation, for travelling, meeting, parting, buying, selling, cooking, killing, and washing of pots, cups, dishes, tables, and person. To rub elbows with a common person defiled a Pharisee. The ponderous code of laws which governed the Sabbath, has been described by the Jews themselves as a 'mountain that hung by the hair.' The Pharisee or Rabbi who executed casuistry, was like to 'a well-plastered cistern full of the water of knowledge, out of which not a drop could escape.'

¶ 18

The Sabbath

The essence of the law, relating to the Sabbath, was the prohibition against work. Business was totally

suspended.   Shops were closed and tools were laid aside.
No fires were lighted.   There are orthodox Jews who still
adhere to this custom, but they arrange the fires on
Friday, and pay a Christian to light them on Saturday.

A tailor was forbidden to carry his needle about with
him on Friday lest suddenly the Sabbath should overtake
him, and he should be weighed down with the tool of
his trade.   False hair might be worn in the house, but
not in the street.   Water could not be taken to animals,
but animals could be taken to water.   Concessions
were made to wooden-legged men and cripples.   They
might tie on their detachable appendages or hobble on
crutches without having the exercise construed as work,
but it was a distinct and unwarranted violation of the
law to cross a stream on stilts.   If a man had lumbago,
he had to grin and bear it to avoid the labour of a hot
fermentation   or   massage.   Conservatives   contended
that broken bones should not be set on the Sabbath.
Liberals said they should.

A Sabbath day's journey was 2000 cubits—about
three-fourths of a mile.   Age did not need as much,
youth needed more, and around this flaming sword
love found a way, other elements found it too.

Casuistry

If they wanted to visit a friend on Saturday, they
hid some food legal distances on Friday, and on the
Sabbath, ate their way across the boundary line, for
the law said, where there was food, there was the home
also!   There were certain acts that might be performed
in the house on the Sabbath, and to do them elsewhere,
the house could be indefinitely extended by means of
strings.   If a piece of glass had been swallowed acci-
dentally, a doctor might be sent for, but if medicine was
to be administered it was to be taken as food, *and with
pleasure*!

The Sabbath was supposed to be a day of Joy!   This
idea was thoroughly emphasised, that the schools of
Hillel and Shammai were divided on the question whether

any one might visit the sick, and by coming in contact with pain, forfeit joy. These examples are sufficient to show that the burden of the law fell with a deadlier weight on the Sabbath, than on any other day. Its net of intricate laws had become an insufferable bore to the majority of the people.

¶ 19

Foreign Influences

Whether the education of Jesus varied from the schooling of the youth of His city and time, we do not know. If it had, we would have probably have some record of it. All boys were taught the law and the prophets. They were taught by an accredited teacher, or their fathers or both. To say that Jesus, however, was unacquainted with Greek culture is a conjecture hardly warranted by facts. The language of Palestine was not immune to its influence, the mother tongue of Jesus was the Syrian dialect. Greek inscriptions were on the coins, and Greek temples and Grecian gods were in plenty. Damascus and Gaza were virtually Greek cities, and amongst the legions of Herod there were Thracian regiments. A youth of the intentions of Jesus could not possibly be oblivious to the changes that were taking place around Him. The Hellenising process was opposed by the Rabbis, but despite the bitterest opposition it persisted and spread. Those who taught their sons Greek science were catalogued with those who raised swine, but the anathema of the Mishna was powerless to exclude the influence.

As He went with His parents to the temple feasts, He saw the strange mingling of nations of the streets of Jerusalem. He compared the various types of foreign nationalities with as much interest as He compared and contrasted various and conflicting mental attitudes of the sects of His own people. If He cast aside reserve to question the doctors, He would with more ease question these foreigners on the affairs of the great outside world.

What He Learned on the Streets

He must have felt as keenly as others of His race, the national reverses that made His nation a vassal of Rome! Everywhere He saw the symbols of their religion, symbols of their civilisation. In the years of national adversity, it was the prophets and poets who kept hope alive in the heart of Israel. In His day there were merely interpreters of prophets and interpreters of poets. But there were also patriotic souls who made the magic words of the past their own: they revived the vivid imagery of the fathers, and gave body and voice to their most ardent hopes. The dominant hope was that which looked for a coming deliverer, who would free them from bondage.

¶ 20

The Messianic Hope

At one time the coming was to be the son of David, and sit on the throne of his fathers. Later the conception changed. He was to be the messenger of Jehovah, appointed from all eternity to appear in the fullness of time, and redeem His people. In the apocalyptic literature of the Jews, we have a strangely extravagant image of the expected One. He was to be a king from heaven endowed with the attributes of Jehovah —yet a Son a Man, and dwelling in the midst of them. He was to be a great Prince who would found an earthly paradise—for Jews. He would free Israel by force of arms, and found a new and supreme dominion in which the chosen ones would live the life of angels, and reverse the relationship that Rome bore to them. His name was to be called Immanuel, the Prince of Peace, the Mighty Counsellor, the Word Wisdom, the Messiah.

There seem to have been a time when leaders in Israel looked upon Cyrus as the realisation of the coming One.   Then Zebrubbael seemed to them to embody the qualities that justified them in centring their hopes on Him.

Before the day of Maccabees, the conception of the Messiah was that He should be a 'Son of David' and free His people.   He was to be their Prince and reign in splendour.

The Deliverer

If the hope waned or the interest flagged, the leader announced that a single day's repentance, by the chosen people, would bring Him into their midst at once.   There were some that said Elias must first come to make straight His path.   He was to ascend the mountains in glory, and make them red with the blood of His foes.   So great was to be the slaughter that the beasts could live for a year on the flesh of the dead, and on the carrion left, the birds of the air could live for seven.   There was to be much and valuable booty, and Israel was to share the spoils.   Sinai, Tabor, and Carmel were to merge their peaks, and on the summit was to be built the capital of the King Messiah.   The houses thereof were to be three miles high, and the length of the city was as the distance a horse could gallop from dawn to noon. No more poverty, no more sickness   It was to be a population of prophets, with visions all fulfilled!

And yet, day by day the potter turned his wheel! the smith fired his forge, the bazaars opened for trade, the hewers of wood, the drawers of water, went as usual to the mountains and the wells.   The tax-gatherers sat in receipt of customs, the money changers in their stalls, the house-wife at her wheel, and the Rabbi pondered over the intricacies of the law.

High as the expectation was—permeated as the thought of the time was with the coming of the new regime, no one thought for a moment of giving up their material possessions as the early Christians did in their enthusiasm of a similar hope. It was a dream in which they found it easier to sacrifice preconceived notions than prepossessions. And yet, some of these same men must have been members of the first Christian church at Jerusalem.

Their minds were coruscating in the clouds, but their feet were firmly planted in the marts of trade.

The background of the thought of Jesus was of the same texture as the thought of the people of His day. A study of the literature which wielded such a powerful influence in the Jewish mind when He appeared gives abundant evidence of this. The *Enoch Literature* written during the last two centuries B.C. is the source of much that appears in the first three Gospels. In first Enoch we find a serious attempt to account for the presence of evil in human history. We find also, clearly outlined the future punishment of the wicked in the abyss of hell, and the tultimate reward of the righteous. The title 'Son of Man' is given special prominence. The coming of the Messiah is foretold almost in the exact words of Matthew 25–31, chap. v. In the *Book of Jubilees*, angelology and demonology are well developed. The Old Testament is silent on the question of immortality. Not so the apocalyptic literature. References to it are not uniform, but the hope of life after death, whether of the good or the evil are a main underlying motive-power of these dream-vision writers, with whose writing Jesus was familiar as a young man. His use of them shows their influence.

Thought Currents

The thought of Rome, of Alexandria, and of Babylonia was familiar to Him. It filtered through, from its source, and was distilled on the streets of Jerusalem and Nazareth, by merchants, travellers, and soldiers. The story of their mighty buildings, their military power, and their civilisations made no impression upon Him. He was more interested in Life. Men and women and children were books and buildings to Him when He emerged from the silent years of His preparation. A single reference seems to indicate that in His youth He followed the trade of a carpenter, but by no hint from Him do we know what He worked at.

¶ 21

Jesus Leaves Nazareth

When He came to the parting of the ways—the way of a worker, and the way of a teacher, which is another form of work, He made no reference to the change. Nor did the evangelists. Not a word about the final break with home and relatives. Whether Joseph was living or dead, we know not. Great gaps lie between one act and another—gaps which can only be bridged by the imagination.

The silent years between twelve and thirty are fruitful fields for the imagination, and men in all ages have penetrated them, but with small results. Men have imagined Him in India, sitting at the feet of her great teachers. Others feel sure that He spent part of His young manhood with the Essenes. His teaching has often been compared with the teachings of both peoples. In the absence of records, we do not know, and mere conjectures serve no useful purpose. It seems fixed in the human mind, that He lived and worked, and died amongst His own people. The rejection of numerous myths and legends concerning His youth, indicate to us that as child, youth, and young man, He lived the normal life of His time.

His Last Night at Home

There must have been some heart-searching moments as He neared the close of His home life. His brothers and sisters may not have appreciated His mental and spiritual outlook, but that could not be true of His mother. What happened on the last day, at the last meal, must have remained in her chamber of imagery as something she could never forget. Let us imagine Him in the late afternoon of that memorable day going out alone to the foot hills of Tabor, to crown the silent years in a communion of solitude.

> 'O Sabbath rest by Galilee!
> O calm of hills above,
> Where Jesus knelt to share with thee,
> The silence of Eternity,
> Interpreted by love.'

As He stood there and watched the going down of the sun beyond Carmel, there must have passed through His mind a retrospect, and a prospect. Around Him on every side lay the ruins of Empires, religions, and civilisations. Within the scope of His vision, the Semitic race sprang into being and passed through all the vicissitudes of national life. Israel, the once powerful nation, was a vassal of Rome. The cities were in ruins, the people were scattered, but in the hearts of those who remained, there lived a wonderful hope. Beyond the reach of His vision lay the ruins of other Empires, founded on force. They came up in glory, they went down in defeat to decay and death. On that narrow strip of land His people had fenced in Jehovah. On the morrow He would begin to remove the fence, and inaugurate a new Kingdom, in which all national lines of demarcation would be ultimately swept away; a new Kingdom which would be held together not by legal codes, or dynastic prerogatives, but by the power of a disinterested love.

CHAPTER III

¶ 22

The Spiritual Capital of Christianity

SEVEN cities contended for the birthplace of Homer. Two claim the honour of being the birthplace of the Son of Man. He loved Jerusalem and wept over her, but her citizens put Him to death as a malefactor. It was reserved for Capernaum to lay just claim to the highest of all honours—the honour of being the scene of the great friendship, the completion of the circle of twelve, and the birthplace of the good News of God. And Capernaum has utterly vanished from the knowledge of men. Its very site is uncertain. It is as if it had never been. It was exalted up to heaven—it was dashed down to hell. But so also was Jerusalem. Bethlehem we know, Nazareth we know, Jerusalem we know, Capernaum we know not.

It was known in the fourth century, then it disappeared. It was the scene of His mighty works, the centre of His activity, and the source of that stream that is still flowing to the ends of the earth. Jerusalem was the capital of the world to the Jews. They preserved what they could of it. Capernaum was the spiritual capital of the Christian world, and was lost to mankind because what happened there was completely overshadowed by theories of His birth and theories of His death. It was His home during the whole of His ministry. Surely, to that place of all others, the yearning hearts of the disciples should have turned in the days when they were bereft of their leader! Its disappearance is another evidence that in the course of

34

what is called evangelical history emphasis has been too often placed upon trivial and utterly non-essential things, to the confusion of religion and the exclusion of things that were vitally important to mankind.

The beginnings at Capernaum were of the most simple character. It was not the beginning of the church as we knew it. It was the beginning of the Kingdom of Heaven. He used the synagogue, but He built no buildings. There was no ritual, no ceremony, no prescribed rules. The personnel of the new movement was objectionable. He Himself was sneeringly referred to as a 'carpenter.' There was hostility against the class of persons to whom He made the offer of entry into the Kingdom. They had no pedigree, no status. They lacked respectability.

¶ 23

His First Sermon: The 'Good News' of God

The earliest Gospel (Mark) gives us the earliest sermon. It was brief and explicit. **'The time is fulfilled, the kingdom of God is at hand, repent ye and believe the good news.'** On that basis He selects His personal followers. The 'good news' was the coming of the Kingdom. All Israel was looking for it and expecting it. They were not agreed as to the method of its coming. There were various ideas. They were all based on the apocalyptic writings of the Fathers. The central idea was the Messiah. Was Jesus the Messiah? Some of the earliest friends believed He was and on that assumption brought others into the circle, but Jesus Himself called His disciples on the basis of the Kingdom. His first sermon is not unlike the message of the Baptist. It is less harsh and more positive. He did not underestimate the value of the religion of Israel: **'They that are whole need not a physician,'** may be understood as a recognition of its value and an indication that even following Him was not an absolute essential. Whence then the opposition? In Capernaum it was a question of method. Toward the end, in Jerusalem, it was a question of personality. To exalt conduct above creed, to ignore authority, to prefer working men to priests, unlearned to learned, poor to rich, and truth to tradition, made Him at once an object of suspicion. While in Galilee He was outside the jurisdiction of the Sanhedrin which is referred to as 'the Council.' This body of seventy-two men was the governing power in Israel. It was a sacerdotal aristocracy usually composed of Sadducees, until Herod espoused the cause of the Pharisees and increased their representation. It was presided over by the High Priest, and held its meetings in the temple. It was the court of last appeal in matters relating to the Mosaic ritual and the conservator of the interests of whatever nobility was left. Everything Roman was hated in Jerusalem, but when the official Jews wanted to get a Jew who was beyond their reach they usually used the arm of the Roman procurator to get him.

¶ 24

Opposition of the Elders: Gamaliel

We are not to suppose that these 'Elders' of Israel were naturally cruel or vindictive or particularly bent on persecution. There were some level-headed and kind-hearted men amongst them. When the disciples were cited before the Council, Gamaliel, one of the leading members, stood up and defended them: 'If this Council or this work be of men,' he said, 'it will come to naught. If it be of God ye cannot overthrow it.' Of course there were not many Gamaliels, but there were probably as many as could be found in a Christian Sanhedrin of modern times. These men were concerned in order, tradition; in minute details

of form and usage. To them apparently the work of
God was a finished product. They imagined that if
Jehovah had anything to say to the world, He would
say it to them first. They were jealous of their power.
Most of us are, if we have any. They probably possessed
as much equilibrium as a House of Bishops would if
they were confronted with the problem of a God-filled
man with a bunch of dockers behind him, who questioned their authority, and threatened their power.

¶ 25

The Kingdom of Friends

In Capernaum, originated the religion of the open
air, and of the open hand, and of the loving heart.
The roadside became a rival of the temple, as a place
in which either to preach or worship. It was the home
of a gigantic dream of a Kingdom of Love, and of a
disinterested enthusiasm for God and brotherhood.
There the world's mind was turned to a religion of the
heart that conceived God as a father and all the sons of
men as his children. In the new Kingdom proclaimed by
the Master, the humble, and the lowly, and the poor,
and the nondescript, all had a place, a destiny, and a
career. Its priesthood was to be composed of a pure
in heart. Stone and brick and wood were no longer
sacred, except as they were used in the service of man.

The New Priesthood

Aristocracy of blood and lineage were done away
with, and a new aristocracy introduced. The new form
was spiritual, and a fisherman or a tax-gatherer was as
eligible as the bluest blood in the world. All caste
was abolished, all social lines of demarcation were
swept away. Breadth of phlacteries and posture of

body mattered little.   There was no altar, no sacrifices
of lambs or burnt offerings or incense.   The new temple
was God's great out-of-doors, the roof was the clear blue
sky, the new gold was the gold of the glorious sunsets
on the quiet lake.   The new sacrifices were humility,
charity, forgiveness, long-suffering, abnegation, and self-
denial, all permeated with a love, that sought another's
good and not its own.   The infinite charm of it all is
still the wonder of the world.

Governments are founded on self-interest.   Patriotism is a virtue, but the vision of the Kingdom of Heaven
showed the world a better way.   Man is more than
self-interest, more than patriotism.   He has a place in a
world scheme, and that place can only be filled by
righteousness that satisfies the soul.   The dream of
Capernaum was the dream of the world religion—a new
Kingdom, the driving force of which was love.

¶ 26

Unity in Diversity

The twelve are a picture of the Kingdom.   Diverse
in temperament, diverse in status, intellect.   Every
one an individual with his own personal characteristics,
but in diversity there is the unity of purpose.   They
are imbued by the same spirit.

The Power of Love

They are as yet unprepared for the larger mission,
but they are apt pupils, and good ground for seed.
Seeds are ideas—the ideas of the Kingdom.   The
closer they live to Him, the better the growth.   They
lie down to sleep on the same floor, they sit around
the same table at meals, they accompany Him to the
solitudes, for communion and prayer.   As they watch
him they learn that love linked to will is manifested
in power—power to heal, to soothe, to encourage, to

comfort, to interpret the father.   He was the door into these untutored souls.

Before they received the great charter, before they could reproduce the impressions received, they had much to learn and little time in which to learn it.   They did not learn it by mere word of mouth instruction. They were in close contact with a divine personality. Sensibility is a subtle quality that almost defies definition.   In general it is the power to receive impressions. Jesus possessed it in an extraordinary degree.   The light thrown on this phase of His character is dim, but sufficient to reveal it.   His sensibility to human feeling was abundantly demonstrated in His warm sympathy with all classes of people, in their needs, in their homes, or on the roadside.   Even the Pharisees were not beyond its limit, for He went to their homes and ate with them. He was sensitive to the charms of nature.   Nothing escaped His notice, nothing was too insignificant to use as an illustration—the sparrow, the lily, the grass of the field.   Sensibility to nature does not alone constitute great character, lacking other qualities it may be maudlin

As Clay in the Hands of the Potter

But sensibility to the feeling of others, and to nature, and to the presence of God are constituent elements of a character that is not only great but beautiful.   The imminence of God was as natural to Him as the omnipresence of Nature.   Sensibility in Him was no mere passive emotion.   It was translated into action.   The twelve were as soft clay in the hands of a potter.   They were individuals sitting at the feet of a personality. How subtle the graduations of light through which the individual gropes toward personality.   They were in an atmosphere for which we have no vocabulary.   We know the cause, and we see the effect, but the transformation is as mysterious as the birth of a butterfly or the colour of a flower.

¶ 27

They grew in His Likeness

Gradually and perhaps unconsciously they found themselves seeing as He saw, hearing as He heard, feeling as He felt. They grew in His likeness. They were not copies. They were themselves plus His spirit. By discovering Him they had discovered themselves. They did not measure life by a book—they measured Him, they measured themselves. They had no mystical vocabulary, no scholastic method of reasoning. He had no such thing Himself and He warned them against the danger of laborious preparation of speeches. The idea was the thing, and when they had that it would always sufficiently clothe itself in words. Thus the Kingdom began, thus it grew and spread from Capernaum, without bell or book or building or priests or money.

These things came later. They came when the spiritual simplicity of Capernaum was lost in the sacerdotalism of Jerusalem. In the course of time the Christians appropriated the Ecclesiastical machinery of Judaism—bag and baggage. It may be seen in full swing to-day in any city in Christendom—priesthood, signs, symbols, phlacteries and all. The labels are changed, but the forms are the same. How strange that the stones of Ceremonialism for which He had no use should become the chief corner-stones in spiritual structures erected in His name!

The only Barrier

Stranger still is it that His followers should persecute and kill each other over forms and theories, when all the time they were all agreed upon the essential truth. He taught, and the simple life He lived. Despite church wars, however, the Kingdom goes on, and the

only barrier to the winning of the world by the Kingdom of God is the impedimenta placed in the way by
His friends.

CHAPTER IV

VOICES HE HEARD IN THE WOODS

¶ 28

The Spiritual Struggles in the Wilderness

IT was the voice of John the Baptist that called Jesus out of obscurity, to the banks of the Jordan. It was the voice of God that called Him into the wooded slopes of a mountain side immediately afterwards One way had been prepared. Another was in preparation John had prepared the first. He, Himself, aolne with the Father, would prepare the second.

We can imagine Him sitting on a low boulder in the solitude of the woods as the shadows deepen, beyond the sound of human voices, far removed from the abode of man. He is a denizen of the woods, where all nature is vocal, yet mute. The bark of a wolf reverberates over the distant valley, a fox in search of food breaks through the decayed branches of the underbrush The birds twitter in the trees as they settle down for the night. The soughing of the wind through the foliage intensifies the stillness. He is alone—alone in the silence, with the Father.

As He reviews the events of the immediate past, vivid scenes flit one after another through His mind He sees the multitude. He sees John, and hears again the thunder-tones that shake the souls of men. He hears the question of the newly awakened He knows their mind. He is one of them. Their hopes and fears are part of His heritage.

Hunger

He had been fasting. The object of fasting is to make bodily interests and desires subserve the desires and interests of the spirit. His long fast has attuned His spirit, rendered it sensitive to the highest calls, but it has reduced his physical strength. The desire for food becomes keen. The wild beasts around Him find food with claw and fang, the birds of the air by instinct find theirs. All that lives in forest, field, and stream, in trees and grass and ground, follow the law of their nature in supplying bodily needs. Man's destiny is different. They live to eat. He eats to live. The wider the gulf between the nature of man and the nature of the animal, the greater the difference in the methods of supplying food to sustain the body.

The body is the temple of the spirit. The desire to sustain it is fundamental. How the desire is to be satisfied is the source of conflict between man and man and between man's body and man's spirit.

The Tempter

Before Jesus had entered upon His ministry—before He had called a disciple, He experienced this conflict. As He sits there He hears voices. The voice of the lower self calls. It has many names, but by whatever name it is called, it is the same thing. It is the power of evil. The Jews clothed it with flesh, and personified it. They called it Satan, the devil, the tempter. In succeeding ages the call of the lower self, that power in man that makes for unrighteousness was made a dogma. Men have quarrelled over its name, and that quarrel itself, apart from the thing discussed, has become a source of evil.

In His physical weakness, the voice of the tempter called upon Him to satisfy His hunger by turning the stones around His feet into bread! The call was definite. Long afterward Jesus told His friends about it, and He left no doubt in their minds as to its meaning. He was possessed of spiritual power. He was asked to use it in a way that others could not use it. He was tempted to use it for personal and fleshly needs:—

'If Thou be the Son of God, command that these stones be made bread.'

If there was no desire in the mind of the Master to comply with the request, there could have been no temptation. The presence of such a desire constituted the conflict. If there was no tendency to obey the call of the lower self there could be no virtue in obeying the higher call. The fact of evil was as real to Jesus as to us. He did not explain that which was self-evident, but He did not raise personified evil to the dignity of a competition with God. The theologians did that.

¶ 29

Good and Evil

Evil is incidental. Good is fundamental. There was a time when evil was not. There will come a time when it will disappear. Meantime it was with Him—attacking Him. It is with us—attacking us. His answer to the tempter is a keynote to His teaching:—

'Man shall not live by bread alone, but by every word that proceedeth out of the mouth of God.'

The Food of the Soul

That is the voice of the higher call. It is the counter challenge of the voice of God. In substance it affirms a fundamental truth! Bread is essential, but it is not the only essential! Bread is the food of the body. Truth is the food of the spirit. Both come from the storehouse of a bountiful providence, but they encounter many vicissitudes on their way to their destinations. There is a way that seemeth right unto the needs of the body, but the end thereof is the destruction of the spirit.

Jesus was tempted to play the magician, but the moral order of the universe is not founded on magic!

The Eternal Struggle

Since men caught fish with a crooked pin, and ploughed the earth with a bent stick, the race has struggled and worked for bread.   Bread is the generic term for the essentials of life.   The struggle for it has been the mother of inventions, sciences, and revolutions.   For it men have sold their birthrights, their ideals, and their souls.   The market is still open, and barter and exchange is still going on—a morsel of bread for a slice of the soul.

The Desires of the Spirit

In obeying the higher call He did not minimise the importances of bread.   He put the emphasis where it belonged.   The 'words that proceed out of the mouth of God' are truth.   The body has its needs and activities. They are physical.   The spirit has its needs and activities.   They are the desire for truth, for goodness, and for beauty, and these are the things that distinguish man from the animal.   There is a truth for the body, and there is a truth for the spirit.   The obedience of Jesus to the higher call does not mean that the food of the body is secular, and the food of the spirit sacred. His temptation is a red flag of warning to humanity, that the evil consists in the means.   He might have proved himself the Son of God, by converting stones into bread, but He would have been infinitely less, 'the bread of Life' for us!   It would have been an exhibition of fear—not of faith.

The humanity which found its most perfect fulfilment in the Master was not given to Him to use as a magic wand over the essentials of life.   It was not an embroidered garment thrown over His shoulders to protect Him from that which was common to all humanity.   It was given him to lead man Godward, and God manward,·

and a monopoly of bread, or of the means for procuring it, is the frustration of both.

Bread is a blessing and spiritual in its nature. When procured by foul means, it becomes a minister of evil, and a curse.

Our Weakest Point

At no point in human existence is the spiritual nature so severely tested as it is in our relation to the question of bread. The fear of hunger becomes the arch tempter. He strikes at our weakest point. He does not ask that stones be turned into bread. He points to a multitude of empty 'hands' and challenges the masters of materials to convert them into profit—and blessed is the man who can paraphrase the reply of Jesus and say: man shall not live by profit alone.

He earned bread by the labour of His Hands

It is difficult for us to understand the oriental methods of teaching truth. They appear to be so fantastic and far fetched. Our western methods are more blunt and matter-of-fact. But, stripped of form and frill, the heart of truth is the same in all hands. However strange the form of the temptation may appear to us, the inner fact revealed the attitude of Jesus to the problem of bread, identified Him for all time with our common humanity.

Bread is a common essential. There must be a common access to it. The gateway must be free.

Labour the Pathway to Bread

Until he was thirty years of age, Jesus proved His right to bread by the labour of His hands. When He laid down the tools of His trade and began His ministry no one doubted His right to bread, any more than we doubt the right of a teacher in our public schools. What

He was tempted to do was to open a private passage to bread through which He alone could enter. He refused for a double reason: first, because we could not follow Him there, and second, because food for the spirit is as necessary as food for the body, and one of the words of eternal truth is that man shall obtain bread by labour! It is as true in the Kingdom of bread as it is in the Kingdom of spirit, that he that entereth by any other door, 'the same is a thief and a robber.'

The second phase of the temptation is a twofold suggestion to misuse power. One suggestion was to cast Himself headlong from the pinnacles of the temple and the other to fall down and worship the tempter. We lose the force of the revelation if we imagine a super-human being with diabolical mind, standing over the weak form of the Master. The conflict is spiritual, and spiritual forces are contending for the mastery. Let us continue to imagine Him sitting there in the solitude, while the conflict rages in His soul. One temptation assailed Him on a present need. He strikes next at the foundation of His future.

The Two Messiahs

What He is asked to do, would not be inconsistent with the nature of such a Messiah as the Jews were looking and waiting for. It is true there were no definite limits attached to the powers of the expected one, but the sacred writings had foretold a wonder worker who was to do marvellous things. He was to ascend the throne of David, and rule His people. He was to reverse the political situation and take swift revenge upon the foreign invaders. Sinai, Carmel, and Tabor were to merge their peaks and on the summit was to be built the city of the Messiah-King. The mountains were to be made red with the blood of His enemies. So great was to be the slaughter that the beasts could live for a year on the flesh of the slain, and, on the carrion that remained, the fowls of the air could subsist for seven.

The pomp and magnificence was to excel anything the world had ever seen. When the tempter offered Him the Kingdoms of the earth he was merely focusing the expectations of the Jewish people.

The voice of the tempter called Him to fulfil the expectation of His people. It was pointed out to Him that He combined in His personality the power of Moses, of Elijah, and Judas Maccabæus. They had done wonderful things. He could do still more wonderful things, if He would. His people would follow Him to death. Jehovah was His God and would not fail Him. There was truth in these suggestions. That was what made them dangerous. He had power. He was asked to test it by a spectacular venture. There was power and glory in temporal things. He was asked to acknowledge and serve this power and add to His prestige and exalt the Jewish state.

The Two Paths

Did He recognise any force in the suggestions? Undoubtedly He did. He saw in them *the good* which is the enemy of the best. Two pathways opened before Him. One led to a Kingdom of temporal power. The other led to the spiritual Kingdom of God. He could see the end of one. It was of a temporary character. The other was endless. In the one His predecessors had become immortal in the hearts of Israel. In the other He had no predecessors. He would walk alone. In one path He would serve a nation, a small nation. In the other He would serve the human race. In one path He saw glory of a kind, and power. On the other, difficulty, hardship, misunderstanding, rejection, and death. He saw power also, not the power to remove the Roman yoke, or re-establish the throne of David, or the power of the sword in slaughtering men, but the greater power to change men's hearts from hate to harmony—from things temporal to things eternal.

¶ 30

Jesus not an Economist

Jesus had no cut and dried system of political economy or ethics, but some of His ideas contain such seeds. These are the phases of life, where we think in a circle. Jesus in the temptation gives us trajectory.   There are millions of people who contend that in the temptation Jesus was confronted with a real flesh and blood competitor of God, but they do not seem to see that a monopoly of bread or misuse of power is a denial of the Son of Man.

He was unwilling to temporise with the power of evil. He could not take it into partnership.   The power He possessed must be used for beneficent purpose only. By resisting evil in His weakness He was putting Himself on a level with the life around Him and furnishing an eternal example to the sons of men.

The struggle reached its climax at the end of His fast.   The story could only be told by Himself.   There was no eyewitness, as in the latter struggle in Gethsemane.   Both were real.   The wilderness was a smelter in which the gold of His spirit was thoroughly tried.

Calm after Storm

When it was over He regained His equilibrium—He was at peace with the world and the Father.   The tempter would return, later, but in another form.   Not to tempt, but with the power of an Empire to strike Him down.   Meantime the vision is clear, the programme is outlined and the fire burns on the altar of His heart.   Blessed were the boulders on which He sat.   Blessed were trees and birds who heard Him sigh. He loved them all, as He loved the world of human beings. He will return to them for rest and quietness, but He leaves them now to inaugurate a Kingdom of Friends.

'Into the woods my Master went,
Clean forspent, forspent,
Into the woods my Master came,
Forspent with love and shame.
But the olives were not blind to Him.
The little gray leaves were kind to Him,
The thorn tree had a mind to Him,
When into the woods He came.

Out of the woods my Master went,
And He was well content.
Out of the woods, my Master came,
Content with death and shame.
When death and shame would woo Him last,
From under the tree they drew Him last;
'Twas on a tree they slew Him last
When out of the woods He came.'

CHAPTER V

THE CIRCLE OF INTIMATE FRIENDS

¶ 31

Simon and Andrew Called

WITHOUT literature, without money, without organisation, without either social or political standing, Jesus began His ministry in Galilee. He wrote nothing, He organised nothing, He ignored organised religion, He ignored the educated men of His day, He used the synagogue as a convenience. He preferred the open air.

Two fishermen, Simon and Andrew his brother are mending their nets, in their boat, by the shore of the Sea of Galilee. Jesus, passing by, hails them. They have heard John the Baptist. They knew Jesus. They had been spiritually quickened. Jesus invites them to follow Him, and they leave their boat and nets and accompany Him. There is no ceremony, they are not asked what they believe, they subscribe no creed. We are not informed whether they were baptized or not.

One thing only they new, and that they knew perfectly — they knew Him. The men who wrote of these beginnings wrote a generation after the death of Jesus. They describe the events differently. Some are almost grotesque in their brevity, others have added a literary atmosphere, but they are all brief, simple, pastoral. **'I will make you to become fishers of men,'** Jesus tells them. They know what He means. They were accustomed to such figures of speech. They used them every day in the common affairs of life. To catch men was to give them new ideas, new ideals, out of which naturally grew a new outlook upon life, a new attitude toward God.

James and John

A little farther along the beach, in their boat, sat Zebedee and his two sons, James and John. They were related to Simon and Andrew. Jesus repeats the simple invitation. They, too, have heard the Baptist. They are acquainted with the contents of His message. They know Jesus. The two sons leave their father and join the small circle of three. They, too, are to become fishers of men, but as yet they are unacquainted with the vocabulary of the vocation.

When the five sat down to eat their first meal together, they looked into each other's faces, and realised that something had happened. What was it? It was a circle of friendship. They were His friends—His intimate friends.

They must have wondered why He called *them*. In the cities around were hundreds of men trained for the priesthood, educated for the temple service, versed in the law. There was a special caste of religious goodness, there were men distinguished in leadership. Why had He not selected His intimate friends from these? He knew. They would learn later.

Working Men

They were rough men, with calloused hands, muscular bodies, and bronzed faces. They were labourers with more brawn than brain. They knew nothing of theological discussions of the day. A group of religious experts could sit all day and enjoy a debate over whether it was a violation of the law to eat an egg on the Sabbath. The interests of these men did not lie in that direction. They could discuss the merits of a hard day's work, they knew all about fish and waterfowl, they knew the signs and portents of the heavens. They loved the lake and the surrounding hills.

They were children of nature and loved their mother in all her moods. In storm and sunshine, when the sea was like a piece of glass, and when the wind howled and whipped the waters into a fury, they toiled for their bread.

Lovers of Nature

They arose at dawn and carried home their catch when the sun burnished in beautiful colours the western sky. They were more familiar with the sound of the woodman's axe than they were with the bleating of the sacrificial lamb. They knew the shepherds of the plains, the tillers of the soil, and the sowers and the reapers whose strong arms provided the people with food. They lived the common life and were of the texture of its woof and warp.

To Philip of Bethsaida Jesus gave the same invitation that He had given the others. The account of His calling is brief. His name and his town is given. He was an acquaintance of Andrew and a fellow townsman.

The more these men walked and talked with the Master the better they became acquainted with His mind and methods. It begins to dawn on them what He is aiming at. In the sacred intimacy they grow bold, and exert themselves to increase the small circle of friends.

A Sceptic Called

Philip had not been in the circle very long before he caught the spirit of the group and increased it by the addition of Nathaniel. The new friend is of a sceptical turn of mind. 'Can any good come out of Nazareth?' he asks, to which Philip answered, 'Come and see!' The genial greeting of the Master, His keen, penetrating insight into the nature of the new-comer disarms criticism and draws from him an expression of faith. Nathaniel was described by the Master to the friends as 'an Israelite in whom there was no guile.' The records, however, would indicate that he lacked the force that would distinguish him from that portion of the group that is clothed in obscurity.

A Publican

The seventh friend came from a despised class—
he was a publican.   As the Master and His friends
passed a toll booth near Capernaum, they saw Levi
sitting at a table collecting taxes for Herod.   That he
was not unprepared for the call is evident by the readiness
with which he accepted it.

It was the Master who spoke.   Levi must have been
startled at His voice, and surprised at finding himself
recognised as a man amongst men.   There had been
some breaking up of the fallow ground of his mind.
He had heard John and Jesus also.   He had undoubtedly
shown a sympathetic interest in the new spiritual movement.   When the Master invited him, he arose at once
and joined the friends.

It is the Greek Evangelist who adds a significant
touch to the story of the publican's call: '*he left all*—
and followed Him,' says Luke.   This was the Master's
first step athwart the lines of class consciousness.   Men
who worked with their hands were *Am-ha-aritz*—the
people of the ground.   They were useful, of course,
but their respectability was another question.   The
publicans were not even useful—they were the lowest of
the low.

That night seven friends sat around the Master in
His abode and listened to the unfolding of His mind.
These group conferences in the evenings as they reclined
at meals or sat under the shade of a tree were important.
They were the schools in which the disciples were taught
the art of the new life.   They learned more there in an
hour than they could from a day's preaching.   Their
reserve could be dispensed with, and they could talk
heart to heart.

¶ 32

The Publican's Farewell Reception

Levi was so full of gratitude that he suggested a

bi-valve through which he could release some of his pent-up emotions. He thought a feast might serve the purpose. He would invite his friends, old and new, and together they would celebrate his entry into the new life. Jesus consented, and the thing was arranged.

Levi's reception is the only social function of which we have any record amongst the disciples.   Perhaps he was the only disciple able to give one.   The Master and His friends were there.   Levi was the host.   His other guests were old time companions of the open road—publicans, sinners, and nondescripts, about whose moral standing there was doubt in the minds of the church people of that day.

In the observance of the minute details of the law, the sinners present had probably left much to be desired. The host had invited them out of the kindness of his heart- They were his equals—whether they had washed their hands or not.   He had pent-up joy.   He wanted some of it to overflow into the hearts of his old friends.   There was no string attached to it, no axe to grind, no reciprocal relation.   It is not even suggested that he had any idea that they would follow his example.

In the midst of the feast, the religious censor arrived. They tiptoed around to find out if everything was kosher.   Of course it wasn't.   Levi was celebrating his escape from the latter bondage!   Their point of attack is interesting.   They flung a sneer at the Master and His friends saying:—

'Why do ye eat with publicans and sinners?'

Jesus Feasts with Sinners

They probably imagined there was no answer.   No such feast had ever been heard of in Capernaum or elsewhere.   It was without precedent, it was in utter disregard of tradition; they had not been invited to discuss it, or approve of it, or even to sit down and share it.

His answer went to the heart of the question. **'They that are whole need not a physician,'** Jesus said, and Levi's inauguration ended in peace.

There is no record of the calling of the other five. In the roster their names appear in the following order: Thomas, James the son of Alpheus, Simon the Zelot, Judas the brother of James, and Judas Iscariot.

The Lesser Lights

Of these only one seems to have possessed force—and that in the wrong direction. The others flit across the stage of a great drama as foils for the leading actors. Their appearances are momentary and comparatively unimportant.

Thomas emerges from oblivion for a moment after the crucifixion. Tradition tells us that James the son of Alpheus was a brother of Levi, and followed a similar occupation. He was called James the Little (not the less) to distinguish him from the son of Zebedee and brother of John. Simon the Zelot had been a Sinn Feiner of Jerusalem. It was his party that brought down the final crash on the Jews as a nation, and scattered them to the ends of the earth. Judas, the son of James, is known also by the name of Lebbæus and Thaddæus. Outside of the roster, his name appears but once. He asked a question and by it revealed the fact that privileged as he had been with personal and intimate contact with the Master, he hadn't the faintest idea as to what Jesus was driving at.

Both men named Judas expected Jesus to make a demonstration of power—not the power of the Kingdom of Heaven, but of power that would confound His enemies. One of them contented himself with asking a question about it. The other made an attempt to precipitate the crisis. Iscariot was the only one who was not a Galilean.

Such was the material that Jesus gathered around Him in an intimate circle of friends. Half of them were unequal to the trust. He knew they were, but

He took them into His confidence and loved them to
the end.   He must have borne much as they became
familiar, and their personal characteristics began to
appear, yet as a family of brothers they lived, sharing
each others joys and sorrows.   They were one in spirit,
the strong neutralising the weak, and the impulsive
the phlegmatic.

¶ 33

Their Strength and their Weakness

The proportion of strong men in the circle of the
twelve seems small when looked at through the eyes
of the Evangelists.   It is well to keep in mind, however,
that what we learn from them is only an infinitesimal
part of such an intimate association.   There were
evidently misunderstanding amongst them.

They were small to what they might have been, if all
had been John's or Peter's.   One Peter was quite an
abundance in such a small group.   The mediocre men
had their places to fill.   We can only guess at what
they actually did for the Evangelists are giving us, not
biographies, but a biography.

The confidence reposed in all these men, and equally
in all, was not a development.   It was spontaneous
and whole-hearted, from the moment He called them
out of the crowd into His immediate and personal
friendship; He expresses this confidence in strong
language.   In addition to that He changed some of
their names.   There comes over us a sense of play-
fulness when we read the change in Simon's name.
We cannot avoid the feeling that Jesus is smiling as
He looks into the face of the rough fisherman and calls
him a Rock!   There were times when he was more
loose sand than rock, but the picture of an immovable
boulder was an end at which he was to aim and ultimately attain!   John and James became sons of Thunder,
Levi became Matthew, Judas, the son of James became

Lebbæus—denoting enthusiasm and warmth of heart, and Nathaniel became Bartholomew.

Mark, in the third chapter of his Gospel, describes what we may understand as the selection of the men whose calling is not specifically otherwise mentioned. Jesus calling around Him a group, takes them apart to a mountain and completes the number—twelve. Having selected the full complement, He takes them into a house. While the Master and His twelve friends are there a crowd gathers outside. A meal has been prepared, and the disciples arrange themselves to partake of it, but the crowd multiplies, and becomes curious, critical, and boisterous, so much so indeed, that it was impossible to eat.

The completion of the twelve and the first assembly must have had a dynamic effect, not only on the crowds who followed, but on the outside friends and relatives of Jesus. The scribes who crowded around Him mitigated the theory of madness by the theory of demoniacal possession. 'He hath Beelzebub,' they said, 'and the Prince of devils He casteth out devils!'

His Relatives believed Him Mad

Why did His friends and relatives consider Him mad? Because by all prevailing canons of judgment He was doing a mad thing. The selection of fishermen, publicans, and nondescripts as leaders in a religious movement was madness. Eating with harlots and thieves and other sinners was madness. To think contrary to the Sanhedrin was madness. To suppose that Jehovah would act through any but the orthodox channels was madness The reputation of His family was at stake. By saving Him they could save themselves.

¶ 34

If He came Again

Sincere souls in all ages have expected Him to reappear

in the clouds.   The Jews expected Him to come in that
manner.   Let us suppose for a moment that He comes—
not as He is expected, but as He came before, and that
in the north country somewhere.   He is born and brought
up.   In the fullness of time He begins to select His
disciples.   Down by the beach at Yarmouth He calls
two such fishermen as Ham and Dan'l Peggotty.   Then
around Newcastle He lays His hand on a miner as He
emerges from the pit.   Then He comes to London and
gets hold of a respectable usurer, who has been fleecing
the poor.   A Sinn Feiner is attracted and joins the
group.   The usurer persuades the Master and the
others to celebrate, so He collects some old time asso-
ciates, whose antecedents are as shady as his own, and
whose occupations are not to be found in the post office
guide.   A demi-monde, a cab-driver, a sandwich man,
and a politician.   Would the coterie fare better than a
similar one did in Capernaum?   Could the ordinary
person who values reputation be dragged there with a
halter?   Can any one imagine a bishop falling over
himself to give a gathering like that the glad hand?
A transfer of scene from Capernaum to London gives
some perspective.   When we know what London would
do we become less critical of Capernaum.

¶ 35

Why the Poor were Chosen

Jesus had an utter disregard for the gangrene of
respectability that stuck in the Jewish mind as a bar-
nacle sticks to the bottom of a ship.   He showed it by
selecting His friends from both the despised and dangerous classes.   All other classes were beyond His reach.
They were too good, too respectable to be of any use to
Him.   It He had confined Himself to the learned leaders
or proud custodians of organized religion, the world
might never have heard of Christianity.   The men He

selected were men of the people.   They sacrificed nothing.
In leaving 'all' the publican left a disreputable job, and
probably much that did not belong to him.   When Peter
said he had 'forsaken' all, Jesus did not embarrass him
by asking for an inventory.   If he had owned anything
worth cataloguing, he might have followed the rich
young ruler into oblivion.   They were poor—without
pride of intellect, or social standing, or lineage.   One of
them became the Zenephon of the movement, but they,
could not all be Zenephons or Bunyans or Boswells
One thing they could all do—they could testify and
bear witness

The testimony consisted, not so much in what He
said as in what He was.   What He believed concerning
the Father, and life, and the future they had yet to learn.
What He *was* they knew at a sitting.   The charm of
His personality, the calm spirit, the wisdom of words,
the deep understanding, and tender sympathy, won their
hearts.   In the matter of witnessing, the poorest intellect
could equal the greatest in warmth of heart, in interpreting, in loyalty, in the utter absence of literature,
witnessing was the all in all.   At the great light they
lit their little candles and then went out to light up the
world.

CHAPTER VI

¶ 36

(1) *A Problem*

JESUS was a problem to the twelve. He was a problem to the Evangelists, to the early church, to historians, philosophers, and theologians of all ages, and He is a problem to-day—a palpable problem.

His Existence Questioned

By problem is meant that in the very nature of things His personality was not and could not be a fixed quantity or a settled dogma. None of the world's great leaders, none of the great founders of religious systems ever presented such a problem. Hundreds of questions about His birth, youth, appearance, and thought, are unanswered and unanswerable. The very existence of Jesus has been questioned of late years. The questioning is a negligible quantity in the problem, however. The result of the assumption that Jesus is a myth has been to bring out into a more bold relief His personality. A sample of the reasoning process by which this mythical theory has been reached will demonstrate the groundlessness of its claim.

A Babylonian Epic

A German orientalist some years ago wrote a book on an epic poem of ancient Babylonia, known as the Gilgamesh Epic. Gilgamesh, the hero, was the King of Erich. The poem describes the adventures of the King and his friend, Eabani. The story antedates

the Christian era by two thousand years.   In a literary
metempsychosis these worthies of Babylonia are made
to live again in the lives of the Old Testament heroes,
and later in the founder of the Christian religion and
in his followers.   The process is simple—the method
used is the parallel.

Ebania returns from the wilderness to his dwelling, the home of Gelgamesh.	Jesus returns from the wilderness to his home.
A plague of fever. Xisuthros intercede for suffering humanity, by which probably the plague is stopped.	The mother-in-law of Peter is sick of a fever and Jesus heals her.
Xisuthros builds himself a ship and keeps it ready.	A boat is kept ready for Jesus.
Xisuthros with his family and friends enter the ship one evening.	Jesus and His disciples enter the boat one evening.
A storm arises and falls.	A storm arises and falls.
Xisuthros lands with his family far from his dwelling.	Jesus lands in Perea, the other side of the lake from His home.
Sinful humanity and most of the animals, including the swine are drowned in the flood.	Two thousand demons or more and two thousand swine are drowned in the lake over which Jesus sailed

The story of Noah and the flood resembles closely this
Babylonian version, but when it is carried over into the
New Testament history and applied to Jesus the parallel
becomes foolish and absurd on the face of it.

Imitators and followers of this German author have

fared no better. The attention they drew to themselves
was the furore a of day, and passed away. The charge
that, 'the example of Jesus (in recognising demoniacal
possession) has been made to justify the most atrocious
cruelties of history,' may not be wholly without truth,
but it is an unfair charge. The burning of the witches
can no more be charges to His example than can the
Inquisition.

¶ 37

His Imagery

His use of the current forms, both in method and
content, was retrospective. These forms are strange to
us. When he speaks—if He did so speak— of Satan as
falling from heaven, and of the judgment of the world
by His twelve disciples from as many thrones we cannot
take it literally. No candid reader of the New Testament
can fail to see that the people to whom He ministered
believed that the world was hurrying toward a catastrophic end. Such a belief meant the negation of all
social values. If the world was coming to an end why
should men bother about the trivial values and associations of common life?

The Catastrophic End

As to how much this view was shared by Jesus the
record is not clear. There are social values in the Sermon
on the Mount, and in the parables. His belief in the
catastrophic end is contained in isolated sentences, here
and there, without sequence. Continually in his audi-
ences crops up the question of a catacysmal ending. He
accepts it. At one time He accepts the 'world-affirming
ethic' which affirms that in God's world men should be
good citizens. At another time He accepts the 'world-
denying ethic' which calls men to separate themselves

from the world and the cares thereof, to contemplation and reflection. Both of these are aspects of ethical teaching, recognised in all ages and amongst all people. Both are liable to extreme interpretation. Over-emphasis in one direction leads to worldiness and in another to asceticism.

If the world was not drawing to an end men were—as far as the world was concerned. Some have seen in the catastrophic expectation a later teaching, but their arguments are not convincing. They but add to the problem. We find it in the literature of the Jews, in larger measure than we do in the Gospels.

Sometimes this idea is confused with the coming of the Kingdom of God. When Jesus is asked for details He refuses to give any. **'That,'** He said, **'is reserved for the Father, alone.'**

Questions of the Ages

The Animistic theory of disease was accepted by people of His day. It was believed that evil spirits entered into human bodies and caused mental and physical derangement.

Jesus seems to have shared this belief. 'If Jesus was omnipotent,' it is asked, 'why did He lend His sanction to such a theory?' We do not know Was He the founder of a new religion, or merely one of a line of Jewish prophets? Did He encourage men to look for a coming Kingdom, or did He teach that the Kingdom is here and now? Was He a spiritual genius or a unique religious Jewish leader? Was He a dreamer who gave His life for a dream, or was He a benevolent fanatic? Was he a revelation of eternal truth, or a deluded idealist? Was He normal or abnormal? Was He startled into leadership by John the Baptist, or was He during the silent years of obscurity preparing for His work? Did He contemplate that His message of the Kingdom of God would later be set aside for the Church? or were the later changes adaptations to time and current controversy and

circumstances? Was He the product of His time or
the Messenger of God bearing to the world God's
love? Is His message as applicable to the twentieth
century as it was to the first? These are but a few of
the multitude of questions that are asked concerning
Jesus. They invade the domain of theology—they are
a challenge to the church, they are not the pharisaic
carpings of insincere critics. They are questionings
of the spirit, and must be spiritually answered. They
come to us as Nathaniel came to Jesus. This honest
doubter Jesus characterised as, **'an Israelite in whom
there was no guile.'**

The truth has nothing to fear from questions. Truth
which cannot be examined, questioned, and analysed
is open to serious question and may be only truth in
name.

The Problem Solvable

Jesus as problem is solvable. The process of solution
is rightly dividing the world of truth. It is getting back
of what men said about Him and what they imagined
He said, to what He said of Himself, of His Father, and
His Father's children. This is the modern trend.
It is a healthy trend and can result only in clearer conception of His personality, His message, and His Kingdom.

¶ 38

(2) As Teacher

The Divine Art of Life

It has been said that Jesus knew nothing of Greek
culture. Without underestimating the value of Greek
or any other culture, perhaps we should be grateful
for this limitation. He taught the world the divine

art of living. That was something that neither the Greeks nor the Jews knew much about. They possessed the forms but they were lifeless. The passionless pursuit of knowledge has usually been accompanied by a vulgar disregard for the culture of millions of human beings by whose labour alone culture is possible. The world's tyrants have all been cultured men.

Jesus shines supreme as a Teacher. Teaching is a matter of suiting mental seed to mental soil, in such a way and under such conditions as to produce the greatest quantity and the choicest of mental fruit. Without knowledge of the soil in which He sowed, a full appreciation of what He produced is impossible. The soil of Israel was rather barren. It was stony ground.

Spiritual Tree Grafting

In His teaching He used the customary forms of methods of address to His people. He added to the deposit of mind stuff around Him, His own contribution and a genius of interpretation that illuminated the whole. It was like grafting into an old tree the sprig of another and better tree. The sprig so grafted begins with the advantage of roots and trunk already matured.

As a teacher, His demeanour was usually calm, placid, and measured, but there were times when He displayed another phase of temperament. His eyes must have flashed with indignant fire when He cleansed His Father's house of the vulgar traffic and bankers who were using the sacred edifice for gain. They have been quite at home ever since, but their immunity is due to our lack of His perspective.

¶ 39

Jesus always Get-at-able

His message was the Kingdom of God. It included an exposition of the nature of God, God's laws, God's

children—their relation to Him and their relation to
each other. He took all these things and wove them
into a fabric, the texture of which was infinitely greater
and more beautiful than anything Israel ever knew.
He did this with consummate skill. It was not wholly
acceptable to all. Various threads were acceptable
to various minds. The warp and woof was rejected
by the theological experts of His day, but accepted
by the common people. His success, even measured
by leaders opposed to Him was great. There are
strange and striking contrasts between Him and the
super-spiritual stars of the modern religious firmament.
Jesus was always get-at-able. He had no attendants,
no understudies, secretaries, or door-keepers to 'protect' Him from intrusion. He was the common possession of all sorts and conditions of men and women.
Social outcasts were as welcome, and could reach Him
as easy as Nicodemus. He was as different from them
in method as in personality.

Personal Charm

The one word that describes His personality more
than any other is the word 'charm.' When I was a
coal miner I once heard Henry Drummond. We—
the audience—were all miners and understood him
rather indifferently, I am afraid, but the charm of
his personality sent at least one man out of the audience
with a new spiritual experience. It was infinitely
more true of the Master, His voice, His manner, His
tender consideration put all people in a mood to listen
and inspired them with a desire to learn.

The record tells of His weeping, but there is no word
intended to convey the idea that He ever laughed. Yet
we know He laughed. All normally-minded people
laugh. The juxtaposition of dissimilar ideas had
the same effect on Jesus that it has on us. The
foolishness of the wise and the wisdom of the foolish
were manifested often in His immediate circle and the
mental gymnastics of the Pharisees and the blundering

impulsiveness of Peter, and others, must often have spread out the thin smile into a wide, joyous laugh.

¶ 40

Mirth

The inconsistency of the Pharisees He illustrated by a word picture. We get it in an outline without even the suggestion of a smile. It is the sort of thing that all the world laughs at. When Eastern people tell a story the words are always accompanied with facial expression, movement of body and expressive gestures. The body talks. We get nothing of this in the Gospel record. Commentators talk and write of the 'joyousness' of Jesus, and not a few books have been written on the subject but a few have been able to escape the spell of tradition and speak of Him as laughing! Tradition tells us that only theologians born north of the Tweed can be joyous without laughing! Jesus was born in a warmer climate. After a series of scathing denunciations He caps the climax with a metaphor that for a realistic picture of absurdity cannot be equalled. He pictures a dignified Pharisee consciously choking on a fly and unconsciously swallowing a camel! A companion picture is that of a man who saw a splinter in his neighbour's eye and couldn't see the log in his own! Jesus was always a good shot at a fact. When assailed there was an instinctive alertness in His parry and unerring precision in His thrust. Sometimes He entangles the Pharisees in their own net. 'By what authority do you do these things?' they asked. Their answer has the semblance of evasion, but a close study of it reveals the fact that they had set a trap for Him, and He replied in kind by laying one for them! **The Baptism of John,'** He asks them, **'was it of God or of man?'** They were wary—they refused to commit themselves. So did He. It is not the highest ideal, but

He knew His people. By refusing to fall into their traps they would be less likely to repeat it, and by offering them one in return they would be forced to see clearly that if they wanted a straight answer they must ask a straight question. The twelve were going out as sheep amnog wolves. They would be quick to note His method with insincere inquirers.

He Teaches by Example

Meeting, incessantly, as He was the intolerable burden of legalism, He was not likely to substitute a new net with a finer mesh than the old one. He never attacked the laws as a whole. As occasion offered He showed the absurdity of external restraints which did not restrain. He did this by example rather than by precept. We occasionally find Him using **'thou shalt not,'** but in the midst of the restriction He radiated a super-personality in a human, transparent way, met each question or difficulty as it came up, then said, **'Go thou and do likewise.'** Working from within, out, was the principle which, if followed, would solve all the difficulties of the law and give satisfaction to the soul. It was the spirit, He emphasized— He pointed out that the letter alone meant death, the spirit meant life.

ᴵ In sending them out, He gave the disciples some injunctions about physical furnishing. He might have summed them up in a phrase, **'When you go out, go as I go,'** but He made it mandatory: **'don't be anxious about clothes, or food, or money. As you teach you will be cared for. As you go into people's houses, salute the house courteously. Don't be discouraged if resented. Your words of courtesy kindly spoken will return to you.'**

¶ 41

Thoughts are Things

Are thoughts *things*, then? Certainly! **A kind**

thought is as potent and vital as a wireless wave winging
its flight—through the air.   Nothing is plainer in the
teaching of Jesus. The word of salutation was 'Shalom'—
peace. If it was rejected it was returned, and was added
to the stock of peace in the heart.   **'The words that
I speak unto you, they are spirit, and they are life.'**
We are learning the secret of wireless words caught in
mid-ocean on the mast of a ship. We have yet to learn
the full meaning of the power of kind thoughts and kind
words sent out long distances to comfort and to bless.
When He expresses gratitude to those who had remained
loyal and true to Him in *His temptation*, we are in contact
with the other side of the shield.   Thoughts may be
malignant and potent also.   His enemies were sending
evil thoughts to Him and He felt them.

The People crowd around Him.

While He was moulding the twelve into messengers
and witnesses, He was doing the work for which the
moulding was a preparation. Men of all classes and
women and little children hung on his words.   They
followed Him along the shores of the lake and so crowded
Him that He made one of the boats a pulpit and ad-
dressed the multitude from it. On another occasion the
people were so eager to be near Him, that they forgot
their meals, and he was importuned to provide food for
them. He seems to have turned occasionally from the
crowd to the twelve and delivered some special words for
their ears only. Most of the personal instruction was
given, however, in the privacy of His own house in
Capernaum.

¶ 42

His Methods

Personality and its cultivation was always a major
theme. His method was the object-lesson, the proverb,

the parable. To teach humility, He takes a child and analyzes the nature of its mind. It is a beautiful picture. The unfruitful fig-tree is made a warning against insincerity. The usefulness and benevolence that knows no limitations is illustrated by the story of the Good Samaritan. In the ungrateful servant who, being forgiven a great debt, refuses to show mercy to the minor debtor, we have an object lesson in gratitude, and when He wants to imbue them with patient hope, He tells the parable of the absent Master who returned when least expected. The lessons are not of the class-room. They are of the open road, the hill-side, and the quiet house-top in the cool of the evening.

We are puzzled by the selection of Judas. Was he mentally denying the thoughts of the Master, while the others were assimilating them and working them out? Was the betrayal the climax of a long series of negotiations, or a dynamic and sudden reversal of all he had learned? We do not know, but we know that Jesus was quick, instinctive, and penetrating in His judgment of men. He gave Judas—as He gave all men—his chance, and Judas missed it. That we know, and that is all that is necessary to know. He was as sensitive to nature as He was to men. No mood or aspect escaped His notice.

God and His World

Ponderous volumes issued from the pen of Calvin in one of the most beautiful spots in the world, yet they contain no hint that He ever saw the mountains or valleys or lakes. Those who wrote of Jesus could not avoid recording His intense love of nature. He knew the birds. His father cared for the least of them—a sparrow. He pointed to the lilies, He spoke of their growth, and said that the regal splendour of Solomon was as nothing compared to them. His reference to flowers and birds, to trees and grass and sunsets, of the fox and his hole, and the lilies of the field, were not text-book sayings—they were familiar inhabitants of the thought world of Jesus. As teacher He was not saying to His pupils, 'Notice my use of nature terms!' He referred to a lily as He referred to God. Both were real to Him, and he was a dull pupil who could not understand. And how strangely this intimacy with nature was forgotten by His followers! St. Francis in his love for 'sister moon' and 'brother wolf' reminds us of Him—and could anything greater be said of a man? Great orators make us think of Demosthenes. There have been great orators in the Christian church. The fire of their words kindles other fires. There have been men of great faith, and they have strengthened the faith of others, but it takes more than oratory or faith to make us compare a man with Jesus.

¶ 43

Simplicity of His Teaching

Paul and John are both great teachers. As expositors they have illuminated and explained many abstruse problems, but we search in vain in the teaching of Jesus for such philosophical and theological discourses as they gave us. It was not the simple truths of the relation of man to God and man to man as taught by Jesus which were forged into terrible weapons of offensive theological warfare, it was the inference drawn from them by His interpretators who were unwilling that other men should view from a different angle.

In view of the complex systems of doctrines arising out of the Gospel records it is remarkable that the message of Jesus is as unique in omission as in content.

A Living Faith

As teacher, He knew that if a man had a pure heart it would be a waste of energy to issue to him a long

series of warnings against women. If every day was a
holy day he would not need the legal instructions concerning the Sabbath. When the pure in heart see God
they need no signposts. Of the millions who crowd the
streets of London, how few there are who know anything
of the laws relating to street traffic. Instinct and
intuition tells them that higher than the law known to
the policemen is the courtesy of the sidewalk. As
teacher, Jesus imparted His personality the chief characteristic of which was a living faith in God. When
that became a personal experience it manifested itself in
others as it did in Him. Whatever failure has attended
Christianity, has been due to the teachers putting the
cart before the horse.

The Value of the Human Soul

Closely akin to this living faith in the Father was
His faith in the eternal worth of the human soul. He
was the supreme truster of men. He saw the good
in them. He pointed out the possibilities in personality.
He saw it in publicans and sinners. He cultivated
and defended it. As a positive force this faith in personality has persisted. No matter how the church
changed, quarrelled, decayed, or flourished, it still
clung to this cardinal contribution—the central theme.
It has not been confined to the stewardship of faith.
It has gone beyond its confines and millions of men
unconnected with organised religion, hark back to
Jesus in the recognition of the worth of the individual
human soul.

¶ 44

(3) As Influence

Christianity gains nothing by such extravagant
claims as it has made throughout the centuries. When-

ever and wherever the trust as Jesus lived it has been tried, it has given new life, and new vision, but it has not been very extensively applied to life. His truth and Christianity are two different things, however.

The bribery, corruption, and persecutions which followed what is called 'the conversion of Constantine' were the methods of politicians to extend an official religion, but they had nothing in common with the Master's point of view.

Christianity and Buddhism

The edicts of Theodosius, dictated by his hireling theologians and visited with ruthless severity upon 'heretics,' were as unlike Jesus as fire is unlike water. The long series of barbarous methods of propagating Christianity in those days were in strange contrast to the methods of Buddhism, which were devoid of such vulgar brutality. As a consequence Buddhism made much more progress than Christianity. Constantine, Theodosius and Henry the Eighth as a trinity of propagandists stand out in strange contrast to the fishermen selected by Jesus in Galilee. The latter were ambassadors of the loving heart, the simple life, and the democratic community. The former were largely responsible for the substitution of priestcraft for discipleship. They turned religion into a state policy and made mutton out of God's sheep.

Jesus and the Child

Christian propagandists are fond of talking about the influence of Jesus on woman, and the life of the child. A British statesman in the second decade of the twentieth century, tells the British nation that an expenditure of two hundred thousand pounds a year would prevent the death of fifty thousand babies! How? By providing food!

¶ 45

Jesus and Business

Millions of little children are slaves of the wheel of labour, hundreds of thousands of mothers give birth to children under conditions that are filthy, brutal, and vulgar—conditions which are much worse than those under which our domestic animals are brought into being. This does not mean that the religion of Jesus has failed. It means that it has not been tried. It means that we hold the theory, but we have not been able with all our boasted loyalty to God to inoculate the state and business with the love which is the essence of the Kingdom of God. Despite all this, despite the multitudes who say, and do not, despite the impedimenta that clogs the stream of life, despite priestcraft and Pharisaism, and rampant hypocrisy, Jesus as influence is a powerful factor in the lives of men. He is a power in organised religion. He is a greater power outside of the organisation. I have heard thousands of men who never enter a place of worship, cheer the name of Jesus with genuine enthusiasm. In the homes of the poor, in the hearts of the nondescript men and women, His name has power. It stands for tenderness, kindness, disinterestedness, and love. Millions reject things called by His name. They accept Him. Without entering the discussion as to whether religion is a universal instinct or not we may safely say that the mind of man engrosses itself with the unknowable as well as the knowable.

It searches the heavens, it tunnels the mountains, it explores vast regions of earth, and sea, and sky. The mind of man aspires. Beyond what we know of either chaos or order we aspire to discover cause. We crave some gleam of hope for a life after death. Here Jesus becomes to us the most powerful of all influences. He postulates that which we are striving to know. He opens a door by which we enter into a larger hope, a surer confidence. For this hope the world is indebted to the Gospels. The truth handed down has had many interpreters, many versions, many distortions, but it is ours, and apart from books or buildings or sects or schisms we secretly cling to it, and the closer we cling the clearer the vision. Nor was the vision clearer to those whose privilege it was to listen to His gracious words and contemplate His form. When the gospels were written there were those who had seen and heard Him. There were traditions which awakened and strengthened faith in Him. In our day we have no such aids. The truth has clothed itself in many forms in the succeeding ages and in the continual change of trustees and custodians. To us, much that seemed essential to those disciples and their successors, is purely historical. But the essence and content of the spiritual experience transmitted from Jesus to His friends, is a unique fact, and is perhaps better understood in the twentieth century than it was in the first

One reason may be that for centuries men's minds have been re-exploring His unique personality. The more we explore that, the more we know of our own personalities, and the more we know of God's. The content of His personality becomes more and more the standard by which we make our judgments, estimate values, and arrive at a new criterion and a new orientation of God.

Jesus the Foundation

There is a healthy and almost universal desire to shelve apologetics and reinstate the experience of the soul. We are all looking for a sounder basis for faith than the varying and uncertain results of critical processes. This sounder, surer foundation can only be found in Jesus, His life, His words, and His sacrifice. We are going back to His central principles, His point of departure, which was love. Love in action—toward the Father and toward men; in union with God and brotherly fellowship.

¶ 46

The Infallible Guide

As if by instinct we turn away from the learned discussions of the theologians to the simple stories Jesus told. The story of the prodigal and his father, the centurion of Capernaum, the Samaritan, heretic, and the woman who broke the box of alabaster. We tire, the world tires of intellectual fencing over religious things. Whatever edification it gave the past it has no place in our times. We never tire of Him, the world never tires of His stories, illustrating life.

The influence of Jesus is so potent in the twentieth century that the desire of the masses can be satisfied with nothing less than the simple truth He taught, about Himself, His Father, and our Father, and the power of love.

Much has been written about the influence of Jesus in art, poetry, and literature, by which is meant, that poets, painters, writers, and thinkers, as they have caught His spirit, have assimilated and transferred it to their self-expression. What happens to the artist happens to the artisan. The influence of Jesus is felt first in the heart. Whether one reads of His life or is influenced by a spiritual personality, the result is the same. The same spiritual forces are released, the same dynamic change takes place. The thought which transforms life is of the same texture that was in the soul of Jesus.

It is still true that the transformation is greatest among the poor. It is still true that there is the Kingdom of Heaven. It is still true that the wind bloweth where it listeth, neither can we tell yet whence it cometh or whither it goeth? So it still is concerning those born of the spirit. Into a rough underground resort for harlots a young woman walked a few years ago with a white rose in her hand. She looked around for a moment and then handed it to a girl who happened to be the most dissolute and abandoned creature in the place. Few words were spoken, and those that were spoken were not pious phrases, but just a winged word of kindly human greeting. The girl took the rose and walked out of the place. Up and down the low, mean streets she walked, with the rose in her hand—thinking. Her thoughts were of the purity of the rose and the kindness of the giver. She contrasted her life with both, and that led her to seek help where the Magdalen found it, and the thought that was in the mind of Jesus when He said, **'neither do I condemn thee,'** entered her mind and she changed the course of her life. As a result she got beauty for ashes and joy for heaviness, and purity in place of sin. The thought implanted in her mind, she implanted in others, and so it went on. Having lit her little candle at the great light, she went out and lit hundreds of others, and the rest of her life she spent for abandoned women, who called her 'the white rose of the Ghetto.'

And this sort of incident can be multiplied by millions. But the influence of Jesus is not confined to individuals. It enters into the great unrest and ferment of nations. Through fire and blood and tears, the nations are now giving birth to a new world. When it is re-born it will be nearer His ideal than the old. And this not unconsciously or subconsciously, but consciously. The nations are now measuring themselves by His standards of values and the twice-born men of the new-born world will re-think Him in the terms of modern life. That which is good and true and pure will survive, and that which defileth shall be cast into the rubbish heaps of things outgrown.

CHAPTER VII

¶ 47

A Working Man in Church

JESUS was a working man. That sentence looks strange in print. It seems almost incomprehensible to us. The gulf is so wide, between classes and class interests that it seems almost inconceivable to us that for eighteen years Jesus worked with His hands as a day labourer.

A celebrated American minister whose name is known throughout the world, told me this story:—

'Yes,' he said, ' I had one working man in my church, in forty years. I noticed him several Sundays, and asked the head usher who he was. The usher said he had noticed the man's evident interest and attendance and had assigned him a seat, but one day he had to tell him that Mr—— had rented the pew for the year. The man never came back. He was a carpenter.'

'He may have been Jesus Himself,' I suggested.

'Well,' he said, 'if it was, he received no better treatment in the twentieth century than He did in the first.'

The Jews held labour to be honourable. So do we. It was the mainstay of their existence, as it is of ours. But they held it to be honourable, *in its place*. That is our attitude. What that place is, is determined by the superior classes today, just as it was then. For the real attitude of the Jews toward those who worked with their hands we must look to their literature. In the 38th chapter of Ecclesiasticus we get this view of labour:—

25 How can he get wisdom that holdeth the plough, and that glorieth in the goad, that driveth oxen, and is occupied in their labours, and whose talk is of bullocks?

26 He that giveth his mind to make furrows, and is diligent to give the kine fodder.

27 So every carpenter and workmaster that laboureth night and day; and they that cut and grave seals, and are diligent to make great variety, and give themselves to counterfeit imagery, and watch to finish a work.

28 The smith also, sitting by the anvil, and considering the ironwork, the vapour of the fire wasteth his flesh and he fighteth with the heat of the furnace: the noise of the hammer and anvil is ever in his ears, and his eyes look still upon the pattern of the thing that he maketh; he setteth his mind to finish his work and watcheth to polish it properly.

29 So doth the potter sitting at his work, and turning the wheel about with his feet, he applieth himself to lead it over; and he is diligent to make clean the furnace.

30 He fashioneth the clay with his arm, and boweth down his strength before his feet; he applieth himself to lead it over, and he is diligent to make clean the furnace.

31 And these trust to their hands, and every one is wise in his work.

32 Without these a city cannot be inhabited; and they shall not dwell where they will nor go up and down.

33 They shall not be sought for in public counsel, nor sit high in the congregation; they shall not sit in the judge's seat, nor understand the sentence of judgment; they cannot declare justice and judgment; and they shall not be found where parables are spoken.

34 But they will maintain the state of the world and all their desire is in the work of their craft.

¶ 48

Slavery

The attitude of Greece and Rome was similar. Rome was the parasitic power of the world. War was her chief industry and slavery was its essence. After each conquest Rome's chief interest was in the horde of slaves, who were marched through her streets, apportioned among the ruling class and auctioned in the market. There were three great sale centres. The supervisors kept the books and collected for the State, the four per cent. of the sale price. The flesh brokers were as expert in improving the appearance of their chattels as dealers in horse-flesh are to-day.

The slaves were trotted to and fro like cattle. They were oiled and rubbed and gingered just as horses are. Those who tried to escape were branded and mutilated with red-hot irons and sharp knives. Every attempt to escape or commit suicide lowered the value. The slaves' power or inclination to keep themselves at a high market value was the means of escape from cruelty. When old and useless they were exposed on an island on the Tiber to die of cold and hunger. Two-thirds of the population of Rome was composed of slaves. They did all the useful work and kept the patricians in idleness, wantonness, and lust. When their market value fell, they were put to the most degrading occupations. Some were chained to door-posts as door-keepers, and sold as part of the building, when the house changed owners. Every man in debt was on the road to slavery. If the debt could not be paid there was but one way out. The creditor took the debtor and sold him as a slave.

¶ 49

Contempt for the Artisan

The contempt for the artisan class was not much different. The Roman view is clear enough. 'We admire a rich purple dye,' says Cicero, 'but we despise the dyer as a vile artisan.' Actors were catalogued with the labourers and artisans. A Roman dramatist who incurred the displeasure of Cæsar was condemned to play a part in one of his own dramas. Said the dramatist that night at the theatre, 'I have lived one day too long. This morning I was a Roman and a dramatist, to-night I am a common actor.' Marcus Terentius Varro—than whom Rome produced no higher type of man—divides agricultural implements into three classes: articulate, semi-articulate, and inarticulate. The articulate were slaves and labourers, the semi-

articulate were cattle, and the inarticulate wagons and
tools.   Plato and Aristotle would probably have similarly
classified Grecian labourers.   They both considered
manual toil and mechanical labour as derogatory to the
status of the citizen.   Zenophon held the same opinion.
His words are almost identical with the words of Ecclesiasticus.   'The arts that are called mechanical,' he
says, 'are naturally held in bad repute in our cities, and
the people who give themselves up to manual labour
are never promoted to public office, and with good
reason.'

Between slaves and free labourers there was an
antagonism akin to the antagonism of trade unions
against prison labour in modern times.   Slaves were farmed out, and the slave holder could afford to do cheaper
work. In the eyes of the Patrician and Pharisee manual
toil of whatever character it might be, and performed by
slaves or free men, was derogatory to the status of
citizenship.

Into that sort of social atmosphere came Jesus the
Carpenter and one of the first inklings we get of his social
status is the sneer: 'Is not this the carpenter?'

Jesus a Master Builder

A carpenter in those days was a builder. He helped fell
the trees, saw them into logs, trim and dress them, and
perhaps haul them long distances, He made his own
tools, dug foundations, selected building material, and
put his hand not merely to a specific phase of work, but
to everything that had to be done in building or transforming the raw material into the finished product.

During the years that Jesus worked with His hands,
He must have covered a wide area.   He came in contact
with hundreds of people who were in similar occupations.
He never trod in the pathway of the priest.   He toiled
along the weary way of the multitude whose lives were
spent in useful work.   It is not at all surprising therefore
to find His speech punctuated with the vocabulary of the
poor, the exploited and the worker.   The hewers of wood
and the drawers of water were His people, and when He

speaks of building a house on a rock, they understand Him when He said, **'Take my yoke upon you and learn of me,'** probably all present knew that one of the jobs He did was to make yokes for oxen. They asked no questions about it. A yoke fitted the necks of two oxen. It was the yoke that made the burden easy to draw, and the parallel truth was that whatever the burden of the heart or soul might be, it would be easier to carry, if He could be a yoke-fellow.

¶ 50

Hand and Brain

He speaks of putting the hand to the plough, of the labourer being worthy of his hire, of the splinter and the beam. 'What is the carpenter doing now?' asked a henchman of Julian the Apostate. 'He is making a coffin,' said a humble disciple, with ready wit. It was purely a proletarian accent when Jesus described the temple as a den of thieves. If he had described it as a den of hypocrites, He would have aroused no antagonism, but *'thieves'* was the word, and He used it. There was one quarter from which Jesus received no criticism. No one ever came to Him and complained that His work as a builder was beneath the standard, or over-charged, or underdone. The work of His hands was as complete as the work of His mind, and there is just a possibility that when He said, **'My Father worketh hitherto, and I work',** that He referred to hand work that was subject to the examination of all those who listened to Him.

He selected working men as His disciples—not simply because they were workers, but because in that class there was a more genuine desire for the life of the spirit. Amongst them there were no parasites, no exploiters, and if they stole, it was only part of what had been stolen from them. They were less hedged about with lies, and conventionalities, by superior airs, false standards, and spurious values. And the sinners of whom He was accused of being the friend. Who were they? They were the toilers who had been worsted in the economic strife.

In His Kingdom, fishermen and labourers 'sat high in the congregation.' They were given a larger place than any others, simply because they were better material. They were softer clay in the hands of the divine potter.

¶ 51

Jesus the Friend of the Workers

The people of the ground—Am-ha-aritz—were the uneducated. Educated fools and brigands had a status. Money then as now was a power   Jesus, as a friend of the workers was powerless; He shared with the workers the stigma of ignorance. 'How knoweth this man letters, not having learned?' they asked. Jerusalem was the centre of snobbery. To the snob, whether Roman or Jewish, the Galilean workers were 'hogs' and 'block-heads.' The wonder and significance of Jesus associating Himself with the 'rabble' has not been fully understood.

The taunt of ignorance could only come from a bastard culture. There was nothing in the intellectual furnishing of a religious leader that Jesus did not possess. He never replies in kind, when the taunt is personal. He never apologised, nor explained. He assumed His comrades as He assumed the Father. He took His stand and seemed pleased to be numbered with the transgressors. As a working man He took His place amongst the workers.

He was thoroughly aware of the social status of labour in Rome and Athens and Alexandria and Jerusalem. He loved the common people. He despised their despoilers. He was courageous enough to defy the standards of the world by exalting men who toiled with their hands. Instead of ceaselessly castigating the rich and powerful, He demonstrated the uselessness of riches and power by training labourers to evangelise the world. To do that He had to cast the tradition of His own people into the scrap heap of worn-out things.

¶ 52

The Workers and the Temple

What a change came over the Kingdom when He went away. What a difference there is to-day between what He taught and what His followers practice. If a hundred working men and their families were to enter a West End church on a Sunday morning they would precipitate a sensation. We have a theory that all are equal in the House of God, but to practice it would revolutionise our arrangements. The difficulty is social and economic. These men and their families wear different clothes, speak a different language, have a different look. If they decided to attend regularly, the regulars would decamp. There is no question of that. What Jesus taught would not for a moment be discussed. The demands of social usage would take precedence of any dictum of the New Testament. Everybody knows what Jesus would do and say, everybody unhesitatingly would know what to do, but only a distinguished soul would dare to act on profound conviction. There are churches to which these people could go. If they were Roman Catholics they could go to any of their churches. If they were Protestants they could go to missions or slum churches operated by the alms of the rich for the poor, and to which the self-respecting never go.

Great cathedrals have degenerated into museums. Great sects into closed religious unions. Great preachers into mere talking machines. The methods of Jesus have been abandoned, His teaching has been moulded into iron bound creeds, and the rich and the powerful, the parasite and the exploiter, are now in full possession of the machinery of whatever religion the world possesses.

If a twentieth-century labourer was asked to describe a modern temple he would instinctively use the same words that Jesus used when describing His Father's House in Jerusalem. The conditions are not very different—they are not different to the labourer.

CHAPTER VIII

¶ 53

The New Birth

WE are indebted to the fourth Gospel for the story of Nicodemus, who, despite the fact that he was a member of the Sanhedrin, is presented by the Evangelist as a hopelessly colourless individual. He came by night to avoid the criticism of his colleagues.

In answer to a brief statement and two questions, Jesus delivered a discourse. That the discourse treats of controversies current after His death is beyond question. It is theological and sacramental. But there are several sayings in it which are characteristic and illuminative of the Gospel of the Kingdom.

'Rabbi,' he begins, 'we know that thou art a teacher come from God: for no man can do these miracles, that Thou dost, except God be with Him.'

Jesus refuses to discuss the miracles. That is significant. The Kingdom is His theme. The *new experience* is fundamental. Without any acknowledgement of the compliment concerning miracles, He tells the ruler that he must be born anew. When he childishly asks how, Jesus gives him an explanation which, if the Christians had remembered, would have saved them shedding each other's blood, and prevented hatred, bitterness and intolerance throughout the centuries.

'The wind bloweth where it listeth, thou hearest the sound thereof, but canst not tell whither it cometh or whither it goeth, so is every one that is born of the spirit.'

In other words the new birth is spiritual, and the mysterious reaction of the divine life upon human life, can no more be defined than the origin of the wind. But like the wind its presence can be felt We know the wind blows. We know the effect of spiritual life. In view of those momentous words of Jesus what are we to think of the dogmatism that settled the origin and destination of the life spiritual and declared heretics all who refused to accept its definition.

What are we to think of the narrow exclusiveness of the sects who to-day refuse to recognise anything as Christian beyond the pale of their authority and anybody who sees the same truth from a different angle? We need only to say that their attitude is unlike the attitude of Jesus.

The state of the ruler's mind seems to have been that of the ancient poet who said: ' I see the better course and approve it, but I follow the worse.' Such an attitude was familiar to Jesus. **'If ye know these things,'** He said, **'happy are ye if ye do them.'** When Jesus pleads He pleads with a city, a nation, or a universe—never with an individual. He never usurped the prerogative of personality. He presented the better way and left the choice, decision, and determination to the individual will.

While Nicodemus was yet in the presence of Jesus his personality—whatever there was of it— had merged into a religious caste. The discourse of Jesus was delivered to a sect—not an individual.

He was not prepared to sever the links which bound him to his official capacity, his reputation and his emoluments.

Jesus does not plead. He has none of the over-zeal of the evangelist who feels it incumbent upon him to 'draw the net.' Jesus outlines to the ruler the truth of which he stands in need, and leaves it there. Over the old man's head hung a crown, but he was bowed down so heavily with the old regime that he could not see it. He was of that vast multitude who, being not far from the Kingdom, never entered it. It was not a matter of doubt or rationalism. It was just common ordinary fear of the truth.

The record tells us that later in the Sanhedrin he made

a point of order: 'Doth our law judge a man except it first hear himself and know what he doeth?'

But when the same Sanhedrin condemned Him to death, Nicodemus does not appear to have protested. After His death he assisted Joseph of Arimathæa to give His body the respect due to the dead.

We have but a mere fragment of tradition that he became a disciple. If he did it was when the early disciples deemed it not inconsistent to be Jews and Christians at the same time.

It was one of these numerous cases where the good becomes the enemy of the best, and the rejection of the highest truth marks clearly the line of demarcation between that which is evil and that which is good.

It was not the mere perception of truth which merited His approval, but the following of it whithersoever it led!

¶ 54

The Little Man in the Tree

It happened in the days of His popularity. He was going along the road to Jericho—the sides of the road were lined with people who were eager to get a close view of Him. Zacchæus was a little man unable to see and unwilling to fight for a place in the crowd. He climbed a tree. There he sat with eager eyes and anxious heart, awaiting His coming. Whatever of truth there may be in telepathy or clairvoyance was as true then as now, but neither was necessary to acquaint Jesus with the unusual incident.

He was sensitive to His mental environment. He could read not only men's faces, but men's thoughts as well and as easily. With keen, penetrating insight into the little man's character, Jesus stopped for a moment when he came to the tree, and looking up, said: **'Make haste and come down, Zacchæus, for to-day I want to abide at your home.'** The crowd stopped, watched, and listened. What they heard displeased them. The value they put upon themselves was high. The value they put upon the publican was low, very low. 'Think of it,' they murmured, 'He is going to be the guest of a man who is a sinner!' And he was. That was His way. He had His standard of values. The crowd had theirs. They were different. Jesus asked no questions. The supreme truster of men knew that this was the first time the man had ever been trusted, ever been recognised, ever been honoured with confidence. Zacchæus is surprised. He makes no profession of belief or faith. The master's confidence produces an instant effect. As a study in values, the effect produced is instructive. Spiritual values at this crisis in the life of Zacchæus were unknown, but the importance of ethical values instantly occurs to him. He hears the murmuring, he hears the charge, the charge is true. He makes no defence. It is not improbable that in the crowd there were those upon whom he had practised usury or wrung from them in taxes more than belonged to him. He knows what is wrong, and the first thought in his mind is to put it right. Restitution is the ethical foundation upon which he proposes to build the spiritual superstructure. In effect he said:—

'Master, what they say is, alas, only too true, but here and now I will restore fourfold to any man I have wronged, and in addition I will give half of all I possess to the poor!'

And Jesus said to him:—

'This day is salvation (soteria—safety, soundness) come to this house.'

In the Old Testament the word salvation occurs about 113 times. In the Gospels it is only used five times. Zacchæus used it three times, John the Baptist once, and Jesus once. In the Old Testament the meaning attached to the word is breadth, enlargement. The passage through the Red Sea was salvation; safety from an enemy, healing from sickness, victory in battle were all comprehended in the word. In the case of

Zacchæus salvation meant his enlargement of life and safety from the enemy of covetousness and greed. The words as fell from the lips of Jesus did not mean what it meant to a later age.

Salvation in good measure, pressed down and running over came to the home of the publican when Jesus entered it.   Significant also are the words:—

'For the Son of Man is come to seek and to save that which was lost.'

Zacchæus was lost in business, in money grabbing, in commercial crookedness.   In contradistinction to Nicodemus, he saw the way out, approved it, and accepted it with joy.

To the good man He said: **'You must be born again,'** to the bad men: **'I am your guest to-day, make haste and conduct me to your home.'**

¶ 55

The Poor Rich Man

'Good Rabbi,' said a rich young ruler to Jesus one day, 'What must I do to inherit eternal life?'

He answered·—

'Why callest thou me good?   None is good save one, that is God.   Thou knowest the commandments. . .'

And the young ruler answered, 'All these I have kept since my youth.

Jesus added:—

'One thing thou lackest.   Sell all that thou hast and give it to the poor, and come, follow me.'

And the ruler was grieved and went away without any answer, for he had great possessions.   It would be just as true to say he was greatly possessed.   Mark adds a tender and significant touch.   He says Jesus looked upon him and loved him.   Jesus could put as much into a look as he could into a whole discourse. By the mere flash of His eyes He must have stricken terror to the money changers. They must have turned live coals when He said, **'Go and tell that fox (Herod) behold I cast out devils and do cures!'** —but immediately afterwards there came over Him an ineffable tenderness and He said:—

'O Jerusalem, Jerusalem, thou that killest the prophets and stonest those who are sent unto thee, how often would I have gathered thy children as a hen gathers her chickens under her wing and ye would not!'

He met the young ruler on the ground of his personal experience and personal character. He had his peculiar needs and Jesus knew what they were. Why did the founder of the Christian religion throw this young man back on the ten commandments and assure him that eternal life lay in their observance? Why did He tell him that God alone was good? Because these were the thoughts that were coursing through the young man's brain. These were the ideals that he held. To his thinking man could reach no higher— this was the mark toward which he was pressing when he came to Jesus. He knew there was something more. It was not very definite or even outlined in his mind, but he knew that Jesus could, and would, tell him. Jesus did. Lovingly and tenderly He handled him. **'There is only one thing more,'** He said, **'sell all you have and be one of my circle of friends.'** Here again Jesus makes entrance to the Kingdom hang on not a theological formula but on what a man is willing to do rather than on what he is willing to think. What he thought could only be tested by what he did. No such test is asked of a man as a prerequisite to entrance into any form of organised religion, in modern times. 'My brethren, if a man come into your assembly with a gold ring,' James said, 'and in goodly apparel, and there come in also a poor man in vile raiment, have ye not respect to him that weareth the gay clothing?' They had, and we have still. But Jesus had no expensive organisation to support, nor did He contemplate any.

Meagre as the report of the incident is, the impression we get is one of sorrow and regret.   What Jesus saw in Him we also see—great possibilities.   Only one thing stood in the way—his money.   Opportunity may knock more than once, but at least once she knocks loudly, and the call is unmistakable.   Two doors were opened to the young man, one leading to the Kingdom, the other to personal oblivion.   He hardly hesitated.   He walked through the door of oblivion and shut it behind him with a bang!

Jesus sighed and said:—

'How hardly shall they that have riches enter into the Kingdom of God.   It is easier for a camel to go through the eye of a needle than for a rich man to enter the Kingdom of God.'

The young ruler like the church at Laodicea (and nearer home) thought he was rich when in fact he was poor and blind and wretched.

¶ 56

Martha's Kitchen-Mindedness

One cry of loneliness, of desolate isolation, escaped the lips of Jesus, **'The foxes have holes, the birds of the air have nests, but the Son of Man hath not where to lay his head!'**   The one relief to this loneliness was the home at Bethany.   That He was a frequent visitor we may assume from the familiarity expressed, from the discussion of the relative values of home life and responsibility.

It is a purely domestic scene, and the only one we have of the kind.   To the sacred joys associated with the name of Home He was an utter stranger.   No cry ever better illustrates the craving of the human heart for fellowship.   During the day He was amongst people—usually crowds of people.   At night He was the companion of men, and men who probably plied Him with questions as children might.   He lived in a perpetual mental storm, the storm of mental change around Him, a storm of conflicting opinions. His own was calm but the process of eternally calming others is a tax and strain on the nervous system that He was as susceptible to as we are. The visit to the home of Zacchæus was an incident. Our imagination likes to play on the thought that after long journeys He repaired to the home of the two sisters and their brother at Bethany.

Of Lazarus we know little. Jesus loved him. That is enough. Of the sisters we have mental portraits, clear and distinct. They are distinct types. In the brief narrative we have their likes and dislikes clearly outlined in a simple domestic scene.

Martha was the busy hands of the home, and Mary the loving heart. One was a practical activity and the other a receptivity. Martha was careful and Mary thoughtful. On the arrival of Jesus Martha went to the kitchen and Mary went to the sitting-room. The division of labour and responsibility was based on experience and understanding. Martha was probably a better cook, but in the presence of highly sensitised natures food is not the only consideration. Jesus needed the home atmosphere and friendly communion. Mary was giving Him that, the comment of Jesus is the final judgment on the justice of Martha's complaint.

She broke in upon them and demanded His judgment on the division of labour—rather, she asked for a review of whatever understanding there was between them. Jesus gave it. Martha was afflicted with kitchen-mindedness. If she had been overworked she could have made an excuse. He would have understood. If there was just cause for complaint she could have talked it over quietly after the meal. It was a common case of fussiness, tinged with a little jealousy. Kitchen-mindedness is a purely flesh pot-dish-washing mentality. Somebody has to cook and wash and sew, but in the presence of such a guest an explosive irritability was in bad taste There is scarcely a home in any civilised country that is not afflicted with kitchen-mindedness—

some fussing member who labours hard but cannot resist
the temptation in the obvious fact, just as Martha did.
'Lord, dost Thou not care that my sister hath left
me to serve alone? bid her therefore that she help me.'
It is a petulant wail that betrays a weakness of character. Kindly He said:—

**'Martha, Martha, thou art anxious and troub-
led about many things. But one thing is needful; and Mary hath chosen that good part which
shall not be taken away from her.'**

And the 'good part' was a quiet confidence, an
evenness of temperament that could serve as quietly
in the kitchen as in the sitting-room. Jesus did not
go there merely to eat. He went to rest, and found
Himself in the midst of what He had probably gone
to escape. Home is an atmosphere dominated by
love, and love seeketh not her own. During His
various visits he had built up in the minds of the sisters
some conception of the Kingdom. He had explained its
basic values, and in a moment of irritation Martha de-
molished the structure as if it had been a house of cards.

¶ 57

The Woman at the Well

Jesus delivered a discourse to Nicodemus. He held a
long and intensely interesting conversation with a Samaritan woman whose morals were off colour. The old
ruler was a man of settled convictions, the woman had a
mind as volatile as the water in her pot. It would be
interesting to know where John got the story. Did it
come by way of Samaria or from Jesus to His disciples?
We do not know. From those who had little He expected
little, and always gave much. To the average mind, this
conversation kindly carried on between the Master and a
loosely-minded woman is extraordinary. A noted
preacher, when asked to preach in a small church in the
north of London, recently said, 'Why should I preach to
dozens in that place when I can preach to thousands elsewhere?' And that about measures the distance between

the Master and His alleged modern prototype.   To such a
man Jesus was wasting His time.   We have a name for the
man or woman who 'wastes' time with such sinners.
We call them missionaries.   To such we give our moral
support and our old clothes, but we prefer a better
dressed and a more intellectual type upon which to ex-
pend our 'superior' energy.

Jesus was alone by the well at Sychar when the
woman came to draw water.   He was thirsty and asked
her for a drink.   Recognising Him as a Jew, she was
surprised at the request.   The orthodox Pharisee
would not think of asking a Samaritan for a drink.
And if her character was known, the ordinary Israelite
would have walked away to avoid contamination.
'How is it that you ask *me*?' she said simply.   Jesus
answered her in a parable.   He spoke of the living
water.   She misunderstood still, and He went on to
explain to her simple mind the truth.   Then there is
a break in the narrative.   The conversation takes a
personal turn.   He asks her to call her husband.   That
brings out her personal inner life.   When she see that
He knows, she said, 'I perceive that Thou art a prophet.'

He did not chide her.   His tone and manner gave
her confidence, and she went on in search of truth.
Her people loved Mount Gerizem, and around it they
centered their system of worship.   Mount Zion was
the rival of Mount Gerizem.   'Our fathers worshipped
here,' she said, 'and You say that Jerusalem is the
place where men ought to worship.'

> **The hour cometh**
> **And is now**
> **When the true worshippers**
> **Shall worship the Father**
> > **in spirit and in truth,**
> **For such doth the Father seek**
> > **to be his worshippers.**

> **God is a spirit**
> **And they that worship him**
> **Must worship him**
> > **in spirit and in truth.**

Comparatively few of His followers have ever quite fully grasped Jesus's method of leading people to the Father.   He had faith in the truth and was ever content to let it do its own work.

In this conversation—probably the longest recorded in the Gospels—we have a new introduction to the Master's mind.   In it we discover that like God He was no respecter of persons.   To say that God is a Spirit is not to define God but rather to indicate what God is not.   The note of universality is clear.   The importance of place, no matter how hallowed, is swept away.   The Father being a spiritual being, seeks worshippers everywhere to worship Him in spirit and in truth.   The human heart becomes a temple, and from it the human spirit goes out in search of the Father, irrespective of time or place or circumstance.   To this woman He revealed the Father, He revealed Himself. He told her the nature of God and the nature of worship. The disciples when they arrived wondered.   The world has wondered ever since.   This spark of love, this touch of kindly intercourse, this recognition of personality fanned into a flame the smouldering fire in the heart of a woman, and she left her water pots and went off to kindle a flame in the hearts of others.

To the enthusiasm aroused He responded, and abode with them two days.

¶ 58

Jesus and Usury

(*An appended comment*)

Usury had been practised for thousands of years before Jesus came.   The Jews learnt the art of getting some thing for nothing, in Babylon.   On the return from captivity, Nehemiah made a determined attack upon it, and forced all usurers to sign a covenant against it.   He forced them to release the already mortgaged property of the poor—and poverty is the mother of the mortgage. Solon performed a like service for Greece and Julius Cæsar copied the Solon legislation for Rome. Cicero tells us that Cato being asked what he thought of usury, answered the question by asking, 'What do you think of murder?' 'If you lend your money,' said Augustine, 'to a man from whom you expect more than you give—not money alone, but anything else, whether it be wheat, wine, oil, or any other article— if you expect to receive any more than you gave, you are an usurer, and in that respect reprehensible.'

'Usury,' says Ruskin in *Fors Clavigerd*, 'includes all investments of capital, whatsoever returning dividends, as distinguished from labour, wages, or profits. Thus any one who works on a railroad as platelayer or stoker, has a right to wages for his work; and any inspector of wheels or rails has a right to payment for such inspection; but idle persons, who have only paid £100 towards the road-making, have the right to the return of £100 and no more. If they take a farthing more, they are usurers. They may take £50 for two years, and £25 for four, or £1 for the hundred. But the first farthing they take more than their hundred, be it sooner or later, is usury.'

Ruskin and St. Augustine may be revolutionary in matter of business, but they are both correctly interpreting the doctrine of the Kingdom of God as taught by Jesus.

'As long as the Church's doctrine of usury was believed, and acted upon,' says W. H. Lecky, 'the arm of industry was paralysed, the expansion of commerce was arrested, and all the countless blessings that have flowed from them, were withheld.'

That is the business point of view, but the 'countless blessings' have not been unalloyed. With the growth of usury, grew the social parasites. In 1290 England expelled the Jews who had a monopoly of moneylending In the course of time the Jew returned. Moneylending became deeply embedded in the social structure. Usury, interest, profit, and unearned increment, became the foundation stones of the entire structure of the commercial world. Whether the tribute to the lender is usury or interest depends upon where one lives. Laws relating to it are different in different countries. What is interest in one state, is usury in another. What became profitable to the masters of materials, became law, and what is lawful becomes sacred. The result is that we are asked to respect not only the law but the result of the law, which is a large section of every community who create nothing, who do no work and base their claim for respectability, and titles on the fact that they are immune from useful toil.

In the Sermon on the Mount, Jesus tells us to lend and not ask back even that which we lend—much less usury.

To interpret Him as endorsing usury is to render Him open to the charge of teaching a lower grade of morality, than the prevailing codes of either Israel, Greece, or Rome! His most violent critic never accused Him of that. Greed and selfishness may prevent us from attaining the Sermon on the Mount, but our failure is less culpable than our attempt to reduce His teaching to absurdity by dragging it down to our low standard!

CHAPTER IX

¶ 59

Basic Principles

BEFORE the twelve could teach, they had to be taught. He had many things to teach them, but they could not learn them all at once. The Messiah portrayed in the Old Testament, and in the book of Enoch, was a wonder worker. He was to redeem Israel, by reforming the law, and restoring the temple. He was to destroy the enemies of Israel and restore prosperity to His people. A new national life had been promised. John the Baptist and Jesus spoke of 'The Kingdom of God.' Did they mean a regenerated Israel in a political as well as a religious sense? The disciples wondered. There was a thin veil of mist between the Master and His disciples. It was still there when the Evangelists wrote their books. It is there now as we look for Him through the colouration, interpretation, and temperament of the writers. Sometimes the veil is dense, the figure is a silhouette. At times the veil lifts or becomes filmy, and we see more clearly. We are not concerned here with textual criticism. We are tying to see Him. In order to do that, it is more important to weigh the evidence than to court witnesses.

The clearest view we get of Him is when He takes the twelve apart and gives them the Magna Charta of the New Kingdom. What we call 'the Sermon on the Mount' is the new charter. In it they are taught the basic principles of life—of life toward God, and

99

men and the world. It is not a technical document, nor a dogmatic system. It is a series of finger-posts pointing the way to God and pure life.

There are unmistakable signs of the editorial hands, even here, but the essence of it is as He gave it. There are separations of text from context, interpolations, and explanations that do not explain, but as a whole it stands intact as a revelation of divine guidance to the Way, the Truth, and the Life.

It is unthinkable that Jesus delivered the sermon just as the Evangelists have given it to us. As it stands, its delivery would occupy about five minutes. He must have talked much longer. John the Baptist must have preached for hours, yet his preaching is condensed to a few fragments which an ordinary speaker could deliver in a few minutes. Questions would naturally be as illuminating as the discourse.

THE SERMON ON THE MOUNT

¶ 60

The Introduction

Blessed are you who are poor, for yours is the Kingdom of God.

Blessed are you who hunger now, for you shall be satisfied.

Blessed are you who weep now, for you shall laugh.

Blessed are you when men hate you, and when they expel you from among them as an evil thing—(on account of the Son of Man).

Then indeed you may be glad and dance for joy, for you may be sure that your reward in heaven shall be great—for that is what their ancestors did to the prophets.

The great majority of critics prefer Matthew's version. They are alarmed at the suggestion of Ebionism (*ebion*— poor people) in Luke. Matthew and Luke differ, though they both drew from the same source. There is no necessity for dogmatism in our choice of records. Interpretation with us, as it was with the Evangelists, is a matter of temperament.

Luke or Matthew—Which?

In Matthew the 'poor' become 'poor in spirit,' and hunger becomes 'hungering and thirsting after righteousness.' He may be avoiding the inference that the Kingdom belonged to the poor because they were poor. An idea that could not have been in the mind of Jesus. But Luke's record is not improved by Matthew's addition. If words have not lost their meaning, 'poor in spirit' means, not humility or self-abasement, but poverty of character. When a man becomes conscious that God is all and he in comparison is nothing, he is rich in spirit—not poor. The church has consistently rejected the Ebionism of Luke and has given us instead the Ebionism of Matthew, which expresses itself in a slavish social and spiritual subserviency and a beggar-whine.

Jesus did not promise the poor monopoly of the Kingdom. He said it was theirs. There was nothing else to which they could make any claim. They were poor because they were exploited and robbed. They were a majority of the people, they crowded around Him. They had hope in Him—they had hope in nothing else. The Romans and the Jewish hierarchy bled them white—now at last they have a champion who, knowing all they had suffered, offers them something to offset their poverty—the Kingdom of God!

· · · · · ·

When Jesus said that a camel could as easily go through the eye of a needle as a rich man could enter heaven, no Evangelist toned it down, but the Commentators did.

They said, by 'the eye of a needle' He meant one of the gates of Jerusalem! Jesus neither excludes the rich from heaven nor gives a monopoly of it to the poor. He states a fundamental fact; that it is hard for the rich to choose the things of the spirit while for the poor it is at least easier. In hungering and thirsting for righteousness the will to eat and drink is all that is required. The food of the spirit is plentiful—while the assurance of even a minimum existence is as yet a dream unrealised.

The Training of the Disciples

In the introduction to the Sermon He has in mind the twelve. He is contrasting the old with the new. He is giving them material for their mission. They will have to face poverty, in their own lives and in the lives of others. They will be hated and perhaps suffer death, but they are to rejoice and leap for joy that they are counted worthy to follow in the footsteps of the prophets.

But woe unto you that are rich! for you have your comfort in full. Woe unto you that are sated now! for ye shall be hungry. Woe unto you that laugh! for ye shall mourn. Woe unto you when all men speak well of you! after the same manner did they to the false prophets.

Luke vi. 24–26.

The woes are the antitheses of the blessings. Luke wrote them as he found them. The editorial hand could hardly make the rich here 'rich in spirit.' Matthew omits them altogether. The introduction thus appears to be expressive of an idea that Jesus expressed in another connection,—'**A man's life consisteth not in the abundance of the things which he possesseth.**' True happiness is not with the outwardly enviable but in richness of soul. They do not tell how to attain the Kingdom, they tell in part what it is. For the remainder of the sermon proper, Matthew's version is taken as being the more complete record.

¶ 61

The Sermon

In five antitheses Jesus illustrates the working of the
spiritual principle and contrasts it with the Jewish code.
**Ye have heard that it was said to the ancients,
thou shalt not kill, and whosoever killeth, he
shall be amenable to judgment.**

**But I say unto you, Whosoever is angry with
his brother shall be amenable to judgment.**

**Moreover it is said, Whosoever shalt call his
brother scoundrel shall be amenable to the
court. But I say unto you, Whosoever calleth
him simpleton shall be amenable to Gehenna.**

Matthew v. 21–23.

Wheat and Chaff

What is there in this section that is new? This:
Jesus sifts the wheat of the spiritual life from the chaff
of tradition and legal enactments. He separates that
which is incidental and transient from that which is
fundamental and permanent, and applies the result to
the life of His day. He singles out motives and shows
their relation to acts. He teaches unity of life by
emphasising the springs of action and relating the
thought to the act. The inference His disciples drew
was that love was the driving force back of all life and
the lack of it man's sorrow. According to the legal code
a man could be cited before the court for uttering a
sneering epithet at his brother man, but for a less offence,
the spiritual principle made him amenable to Gehenna—
the smouldering rubbish heap of Hinnom.

¶ 62

Of Impure Thought

**Ye have heard that it was said, Thou shalt not
commit adultery.**

But I say unto you, Every one that looketh on a woman lustfully hath already committed adultery with her in his heart.

Moreover it is said, Whoso putteth away his wife, must give her a certificate of divorce.

But I say unto you, every one that putteth away his wife committeth adultery.

And whoso married her that was divorced, committeth adultery.

Matthew v. 27–32.

Jesus is dealing here with the thought behind the act. There is no moral difference between the desire that lacks only opportunity and the act itself. He is not enacting a legal code. He is contrasting the law of the spirit with the Eighth Commandment. Matthew, editorially adds, 'except for fornication.' Neither Luke nor Mark know anything of this limitation and the spiritual principle excludes it. The interpolation is legalistic. It codifies the principle.

Divorce

Jesus explains elsewhere why Moses permitted divorce. It was to prevent worse evils. Men's hearts were hard. and Moses legislated for conditions as he found them. He does not criticise Moses, He enunciates a higher law —the law of love. In the days of Moses divorce was a man's convenience. Woman appears to be the only property he wanted to get rid of. Jesus is not enacting another mosaic code. He is preching the unity of life and interpreting the higher law which obviates the necessity of a barbed wire fence of legal enactments. In the new law of love women acquire a new status, They become equals and independent. He does not enact a new divorce law. He holds the ideal. Men have tried to make the Sermon on the Mount a codicil to the will of Moses, but the attempts have always failed. Because of the hardness of men's heart spolitical creeds and constitutions are still mosaic and when put in parallel columns with the Sermon on the Mount look devoid of spiritual content. At best the justice in them is a balanced selfishness. In the spiritual constitution of the new society self is eliminated and men desire the good because it is good and for no other reason. Legislation on divorce may be as necessary now as it was in the days of Moses. Jesus shows the better way.

¶ 63

Untruthfulness and the Law against Perjury

Again ye have heard that it was said to the ancients, Forswear not thyself, but perform thine oaths to the Lord.

But I say unto you, Swear not at all: Neither by heaven, for it is God's throne.

Nor by the earth, for it is his footstool.

Nor by Jerusalem, for it is the city of the great King;

Neither by thy head, for thou canst not make one hair white or black.

But let your yea be yea and your nay be nay. What exceedeth this is from the Evil One.

Matthew v. 33–37.

Casuistry and Lying

There was a variety of ways in which the law against false swearing or perjury could be evaded. The more sacred the name attached to an affirmation of veracity of innocence the more credence it was expected to receive. If a man sold an ass and the buyer discovered later that it was defective, and complained, the seller would swear with uplifted hand that it was whole and without blemish when he sold it He would use the word that he thought would most impress the duped buyer—the Temple, Jerusalem, the Earth, or Jehovah Himself. Jesus is here announcing the philosophy of the spirit which desires truth for its own sake. He is condemning casuistic mendacity, whether in social intercourse or commercial dealings, and pointing out that the life of God in the soul obviates the necessity of a lying circumlocution. This section has a special meaning for modern secret diplomacy and commercial correspondence — and particularly for our brazen untruthfulness in advertising. If politics and business would cease common lying for one week, the effect would precipitate a revolution the like which the world has never seen. There is a sidelight here on 'blessed are ye poor.' The less we possess the less we have to lie about. A lie is a lie whether it is acted, lived, written, or told, and the only law that can successfully deal with it is the law of the Kingdom in the heart.

¶ 64

Non-resistance and the Limitation of Retaliation

Ye have heard that it was said, an eye (only) for an eye.

And a tooth (only) for a tooth.

But I say unto you, resist not the violent.

To him that smiteth thee on the one cheek, offer also the other.

And if any would sue thee and take thy cloak, let him have thy tunic as well.

And whoso would impress thee for one mile go with him two.

Give to him that asketh, and from him that would borrow turn not away.

So whatsoever ye would that men should do unto you, do even so unto them.

> *Matthew* v. 38–39.
> *Luke* vi. 27.
> *Matthew* v. 40–41.
> *Matthew* vii. 12.

Facts and Theories

Six basic qualities of life are enunciated here. Of all

the principles laid down by Jesus, the first is the least understood and the last is the least practised. One is the principle of non-resistance and the other is the golden rule. In them lies the root of the matter. In a world war the question of non-resistance is highly accentuated. Nobody in Europe at this moment is beyond the possibility of death from violence. Confronted with a fact our theories are in the crucible. As a nation we are forced to choose between annihilation or vassalage and resistance. The individual is also driven to make a choice between acquiescence in the national will and resistance. The determining factor in the choice of the nation is partly a love of ancient landmarks and partly fear of subservience to a brutal foreign power. The determining factor in the choice of the individual is the ethical consideration involved in resisting the violent and returning evil for evil. The national will makes provision for the individual conscience. The provision has limitations. It may be ethical in intent and unethical in execution. The national will when confronted with national extinction gives scant attention to individual considerations. The non-resistent is confronted with a real difficulty. He has to decide the difference between resisting the national will and refusing to resist a foreign invader. In the face of such difficulty it seems unwise to dogmatise overmuch. There is in all of us a deep-rooted conviction, however, that war is a violation of both the letter and spirit of the Sermon on the Mount. All nations at war have for the moment shelved it. We seem to have descended to a lower ethical plane. We cannot reconcile human slaughter with the character of Jesus and the love of God. On the other hand, we cannot believe that God is detached or that He has abandoned men. God will not rend the heavens and come down. We have the prerogative of choice and at present we seem to have chosen not the highest but the lesser of two evils. Whatever the ultimate truth may be for a nation there can be no question about the intent of the words of Jesus as they relate to the individual.

Non-Resistance

Personal insults and violence towards the person are not to be resisted. Personal non-resistance is the better policy even if it utterly lacked an ethical principle. The question of the smitten cheek covers the category of personal insult. It is the question of war reduced to the belligerency of two. It is a more severe test of the spirit than war is. It comes nearer home. By the law of the Kingdom, retaliation is outlawed, revenge has no place. It is assumed here, of course, that non-resistance is determined by a principle and not by cowardice.

A Pyramid on its Apex

Some of our great religious teachers have recently told us that this injunction cannot be carried out, 'without upsetting the whole basis of society.' That is exactly what Jesus intended to do. Upset the basis of society as He found it and as it exists to-day. In apostolic times it was charged against the apostles that they were 'turning the world upside down.' Unhappily they did not succeed, but from the standpoint of Jesus and His followers until it is turned upside down it will never be right side up! It is like a pyramid on its apex and must be thrown over on its base. It can only be done by a love that exceeds the love of either ancient or modern Pharisees. There is no ethical difference between resisting an invading host and resisting a staggering blow to our personal vanity or our alleged dignity. We can choose the plane on which we live. We can prefer the methods of the Kaiser to the methods of Jesus, but they are not interchangeable. The ideals rose still higher, when Jesus tells them that when a man to whom they are indebted takes away the outer coat—which the law permits—that they are to offer also the inner tunic, which the law forbids. That strikes deeper at the roots of existence If a man forces one to accompany him one mile, he is to offer to travel an extra one, because only in the second mile can he demonstrate that he belongs to the Kingdom. We are to give until there is nothing left, lend until there is nothing left to borrow. Hard sayings to those who have anything either to give or lend, but they are sayings of One who Himself had absolutely nothing to give but love. Perhaps that is the normal condition of those who accept the new law as a rule of life—blessed are ye poor, for yours is the Kingdom of God

The Kingdom in Action

These basic values rise still higher in the last clause. When the heart is pure, the self-life reduced to a minimum and the driving force is disinterested love—even then negation misses the mark. The law of the Kingdom is a positive force. It does not hang around awaiting emergencies, it goes out to borrow trouble, to lend love, to share its comforts, and walk extra miles. **'Whatsoever ye would that men should do to you do ye even so to them'**—don't wait for them as they wait for you! That's the old way. Go out and seek them! It takes love and courage to do that, but anything less falls short of the Kingdom.

¶ 65

Kindness—Limited and Unlimited

Ye have heard that it was said, Love thy neighbour and hate thine enemy.

But I say unto you, Love your enemies, and pray for them that persecute you;

That ye may be the sons of your Father in heaven. For he maketh his sun to rise on both wicked and good.

And the rain to fall on just and unjust.

For if ye love them that love you, what credit have ye?

Do not the very tax-gatherers the same?
And if ye say, 'God be with you' to your breth-
ren only, what credit have ye?
Do not the very Gentiles the same?
But love your enemies, and do good and lend
without hope of return,
And your reward shall be great, and ye shall
be the Sons of the Highest;
For he is kind even to the unthankful and the
wicked.
Ye therefore shall be complete in goodness,
As your Father in heaven is complete.

Matthew v 43–45 and 48.
Luke vi. 35.

In some of the Psalms (109 for instance), we have
the only instances in which hatred of an enemy finds
sanction in Hebrew literature or law. Even there it
is a poetic rhapsody to emphasise the distinction between
virtue and vice. Hatred of an enemy was assumed, as it
is with us, but it was nowhere commanded. Jesus here
is employing the Jewish and oriental method of teaching
by contrast just as He was when He seemed, or seems
to our Western matter-of-fact standard of judgment, to
be inculcating hatred of kindred, 'father, mother, wife,
children, brethren, and sisters,' when He was merely
emphasising by contrast the more fundamental claims of
the Kingdom.

Courtesy

To greet the brethren with kindly salutation 'Shalom!'
was a courtesy of which they had no monopoly. The
Gentiles were as courteous to each other.

To say 'Shalom' (peace) to those who persecuted
them and despitefully used them, was a demonstration
of that which distinguished the Kingdom from the
world. Even then, if done in a perfunctory manner,
it was without commendation or merit. To do good,
to give, to lend without hope of return in kind or interest,

to do it because it was good to do, because it was the natural overflowing of a full heart, was an evidence that they were sons of the Highest.

And the doing would become a habit and that habit would become a destiny, and their destiny was nothing short of the completeness with which they contemplated the Father in heaven. Such were the methods of culture, such was the ultimate belief of the charmed circle of friends through which the water of life would overflow the earth. The kindheartedness of thieves, thugs, and harlots is proverbial—as proverbial as the Pharisaism of religious leaders. For the former Jesus had the tenderest pity, for the latter he had extreme scorn. The tax-gatherer's standard of love is not sufficient, however. The Kingdom's credential is the higher love, the love that can love the unlovely and the unloving, that can pray for them and forgive them; a love which in essence is of the same texture as the love of God.

¶ 66

Spiritual Eclipse

Just now we are breaking under the strain of the test. We are loving our enemies by gun and sword, by liquid fire and asphyxiating gas. Our enemy in the name of God, is doing the same to us. The only regret that either of us possess is the regret that the machinery of death cannot keep pace with the will to kill. The world is suffering from aberration of the mind, and an almost total eclipse of ethical consideration. It is a temporary condition. Those who are left will recover. Meantime there stands the eternal standard which demands a love that exceeds the love of the unethical, and the unmoral elements of society, that lay claim to no spiritual heritage or connection whatever.

Worship: True and False

(First Anthithesis)

Almsgiving

Take heed of your acts of piety, that ye do them not before men to be seen of them, otherwise ye have no reward with your Father in heaven.

Thus when thou art giving alms, make not a flourish of trumpets as do the hypocrites in the synagogue and on the streets. That ye may be honoured of men. Of a truth I say unto you that they have their receipt in full.

But thou when thou art giving alms, let not thy left hand know what they right hand is doing, that thine alms may be in secret; and thy Father which seeth in secret shall recompense thee.

Matthew vi. 2–4.

(Second Antithesis)

Prayer

And when ye are praying be not like the hypocrites; for they love to stand and pray in the synagogues and on the street corners that they may be seen of men.

Of a truth I say unto you that they have their reward in full.

But thou when thou prayest, enter into the inner room and shut the door and pray in secret to thy Father, and thy Father which seeth in secret shall recompense thee.

Matthew vi. 5.

(Third Antithesis)

Fasting

But when thou are fasting be not like the hypocrites wry faced, for they disfigure their

**faces that they may figure as fasting before men.
Of a truth I say unto you they have their reward
in full.   But when thou art fasting annoint thy
head and wash thy face that thou appear not
as a faster unto men, but unto thy Father (that
is in secret) and thy Father (that seeth in secret)
shall recompense thee.**

Matthew vi. 16–18.

¶ 67

Church Parades

In this section we have three antitheses and a principle.   The principle is that worship of God must be
performed in spirit and in truth—as unto God and
not unto men.   Whatever outward show the people
of that day were prone to effect in worship, Jesus draws
a distinction between it and the attitude of the heart.
It is not quite clear what it is, but it was probably something like our full dress parades on Sundays.   Attitude
of the heart alone merits God's reward.   Fine clothes,
pre-empted front pews and all the pomp and vulgar
display of wealth represented in jewellery, millinery, and
costly attire, may harmonise with the church furniture
and minister to the æsthetic sense, but it is not worship.
Man looketh upon the outward appearance, and we take
scrupulous care that he has a weekly view at the best
we have.   God may be interested in these things, but
He cannot be pleased with a display of clothes that
subjects the poor to such a violent contrast that they
are conspicuous by their absence in the house of prayer.
The law of the Kingdom is not based on a *quid pro
quo* (the giving of one thing for another of equal value)
arrangement.   Religion is not stock-broking nor is
it an investment.   It is not marketable.   God does
not reward, but to worship for gain is the negation of
religion.

'Would that I could blot out heaven
And quench hell,
That men might love God
For His own sake.'

Our Benevolent Feudalism

The first antithesis is a metaphor illustrating right and wrong methods of giving alms. 'A flourish of trumpets,' is a picture of a hypocrite calling attention to himself. We do it more subtly and on a larger scale. Our trumpets are newspapers and our alms are universities, libraries, church windows and organs, and occasionally a cathedral. A steel merchant gets a prohibitive tariff on his commodity, and works thousands of men fourteen hours a day and seven days a week on starvation wages until he amasses millions. Then he gives it back, not to the workers, but to the more intelligent portion of the community in the form of libraries.

A brewer succeeds in his business beyond his dreams and with his profits builds a cathedral. When these trumpets are blown we all stand aghast with our hands extended for what we receive are devoutly thankful. Jesus said, **'I say unto you they have their reward in full.'** A critic has translated that as follows— 'they have their receipt in full,' which may mean that we give them honour while those coming after us and seeing the ethical relation of things more clearly will be ashamed of the heritage of such alms. Both in almsgiving and in evangelisation we exploit the recipients of our service. Lacking faith in God to provide funds, we hire literary men to write up harrowing details of poverty, destitution, and neglect. The worse the case the better for the appeals for funds. When a sinner changes his course we do the same with him. We omit the details in print but we whisper them around and hope thereby to increase sympathy for our work and incidentally to raise the estimate of our own value as winners of souls.

¶ 68

How the Right Hand informs the Left

The rarest thing in religious life is a right hand that does not appoint a committee to inform the left of its philanthropy. Almsgiving is a passing phase of civilisation. It is degrading, in large measure, both to the giver and the given. When his charter becomes the law of life there will be no almsgiving—nor will there be any need of a church.

.   .   .   .   .

The second antithesis concerns right and wrong methods of prayer. The religious hypocrite displayed his religious wares in the open. The object was to be seen of men. Men gave him a certain kind of reverence. That was his 'receipt in full,' but the Father rewarded him on the plane of his motive. It was low, and the reward was correspondingly low. Prayer is not a religious mendicancy. It is not a beggar whine for a few miserable gratuities.

Prayer an Atmosphere

Prayer is an attitude. It is an atmosphere. It is communion—the attitude of a child toward a father, an atmosphere of reverence and love, a communion of the spirit with the over-spirit—God. The prayer of the right motive and right atmosphere is rewarded by culture of spirit, by clearness of vision, by divine assurance, divine communion. The soul that thus communes with God does not ask for things. It does not need to do so. The Father knows and supplies.' This was the method of Jesus. This is what He taught His followers.

¶ 69

The Temple of the Body

The third antithesis concerns true and false fasting. Jesus was not as strict in fasting as John the Baptist

was, but he practised it and taught its value. He
laid down no rules for its observance. He stated a
principle and left it to the individual to decide how and
when he should bring his body under control so that
the physical condition would be a help and not a hin-
drance to the spirit. The body also is spiritual. Pam-
pered, glutted, and sated, it becomes logy, flaccid, and
inert. It can be so overcrowded with food as to leave
no room for the spirit. **'Don't fast as do these long-
faced hypocrites,'** Jesus says. He urges them and
us to fast as we pray and as we give alms. In the heart,
impelled by a sacred motive as unto the Father. If we
perform a dumb show we have our reward in the show—
a hollow approbation by hollow-minded men. Out of
this principle the church forged a hard, iron-bound creed.
It instituted an intensive fasting campaign of six weeks
and banished by inference the whole question for the
rest of the year.

¶ 70

The Principle Applied

**Judge not, that ye be not judged; for with
what judgment ye judge he shall be judged
(and in what measure ye measure out, it shall
be measured back to you).**

**But why regardest thou the splinter in thy
brother's eye, but consider thou not the beam
in thine own eye?**

**Or wilt thou say to thy brother, let me re-
move the splinter from thine eye, and lo there
is a beam in thine own eye?**

**Hypocrite, remove first the beam from thine
own eye and then thou shalt see clearly to remove
the splinter from thy brother's eye.**

¶ 71

How to Judge

When Jesus whipped the money changers from the
temple it may be presumed that He was not only judging

them but executing judgment. He judged them as
everybody did, by their fruits. In view of that incident
the absolute statement is subject to qualifications. The
injunction is another version of the golden rule. We are
to judge with the judgment that we would like to be
judged and to the man who is about to judge us we would
like to say: 'Before you judge me, get the motives.
Don't judge me by appearance, or hearsay, or rumour.
Make some allowance for my individual point of view.
Reserve your judgment until you know all the facts,
and even then temper it with mercy and kindness.
Put yourself in my place and as you judge remember
that my final judge is God.' What is forbidden is not
judgment, but unfair judgment and the context shows
that before we judge another we must judge ourselves.
Before we can remove the splinter from a brother's eye
we must remove the beam from our own.

This is the Master's plea for the sinner. The man
who has succumbed to temptation, and was then, as
he is now subjected to ostracism and humiliation by the
self-righteous.

**A good tree cannot bear bad fruit, nor a rotten
tree produce good fruit.**

**Either make the tree good and its fruit good,
or make the tree rotten and its fruit rotten.**

**The good man from his good store bringeth
forth good things, and the evil man from his
evil store bringeth forth evil things.**

The power of the Kingdom is in the heart. All
reform must begin there. The fruit of the pure heart
is loving kindness, tender mercy, long suffering, fair
play, and consideration. The fruit of the other kind is
malice, jealousy, hatred, and censoriousness. When the
human heart is the garden of God there will be no doubt
about the flowers and fruit.

¶ 72

Talk and Action

And why call ye me Lord, Lord and do not the things which I say?

A Parable in Illustration

Every one that heareth my words and doeth them shall be likened to a wise man that built his house upon a rock.

The rain poured down, the floods came, the winds blew, and beat upon that house, and it fell not; for it was founded on the rock.

And every one that heareth my words and doeth them not shall be likened to a foolish man that built his house on the sand.

The rain poured down, the floods came, the winds blew and beat upon that house, and it fell, and the fall thereof was great.

Heresy and Truth

The heresy which has corrupted the church in all ages is not theological but moral—it is saying one thing and doing another. We are still saying, 'Lord, Lord,' and on mere profession we have built a pious superstructure which, like the house built upon the sand, must ultimately be swept away. There is but one sure foundation. It is the truth of His charter, held, not merely as an intellectual concept but as a rule of life. Not something that can be put on and taken off as a garment, but something woven into the very texture of character.

¶ 73

The Postlude

And it came to pass when Jesus had finished these sayings, the crowds were amazed at His teaching; for

His way of teaching them was as one that has authority, and not as their scribes.

He begins with the twelve and ends with the multitude. The discrepancy in the record, if there is one, is immaterial. Crowds followed Him everywhere. We get but an infinitesimal part of what He said, but we get the fundamentals—we get the charter. The authority that astounded them was inherent in His personality. It was not that He said anything new, but that His words were living things and conveyed life.

¶ 74

Review of the Charter

Spiritual Exploration

Primarily the discourse was for the twelve. It was their seminary course. If the multitude did not get it at first hand they got it later. Its ultimate destination was the world. In the introduction He announces that happiness is possible to those who suffer. The condition of happiness is in character. There is a new exploration of the continent of God's grace. New discoveries are made. New possibilities emphasised. He congratulates the poor. The Kingdom is theirs in a special sense. The rich are not excluded but they are not to be envied. They are accepted for what they are, not for what they possess. He that accepts the Kingdom is rich. He that rejects it is poor. The false prophets were honoured of men. The true prophet will be rejected of men, but he will be honoured of God. The evil thought is as criminal as the evil deed. The law of the Kingdom is summed up in a word—love.

How the Law Works

When love to God and love to man dominates the heart, the tongue will utter no sneer, it will not accuse, its speech will be plain and clean. The old régime permitted divorce because men's hearts were hard. The new law lifting men out of the dominion of the material sense will obviate the necessity that Moses was forced to concede. The old Torah had failed. The new principle was to be put into force. Personal violence was not to be resisted. It was to be met with love, and love would conquer. The casuistry and trickery of holy phrases was to give place to a plain yes or no. Those who had the real spirit of the new law could test it by their willingness to lend, to give away, to oblige, to forgive, to love an enemy, to pray for persecutors. Sonship was to be proven by simplicity of life. To desire little makes poverty equal to riches and no court could levy a tax on spiritual wealth.

¶ 75

Unity of Life in God

The new idea of prayer was communion. That is a matter, not of standing at the street corners with folded hands, or in the temple either—it was a matter of the heart and it must be performed without ostentation. Current types of piety are contrasted with the new principle of loving duty to God. Good deeds are to be done quietly, modestly, and in secret. The new life was to be exemplified by preferring one another, by the elimination of selfish desires and personal ambitions. By these means the old nature was changed and the new tinaugurated. Unity of life was perfected by the spiriual union of the soul with God and when the nexus was complete they would stand in their new relation like the house that was built on the rock. The foundation was firm and solid. The superstructure could not be shaken. When these sayings had sunk deep into their hearts and they had woven it into the fibre of their personalities, they went out to give the world the most complete and efficient remedy for world weariness, distraction, poverty, misery, and sin that the race has ever known. To the dullest existence the door of heaven opens and light comes forth.

This, then, is the Master's Magna Charta. A series of new requirements for the spiritual life that were set against the old Torah. It is not a new decalogue in the legal sense. It is a new interpretation of life.

¶ 76

The Faith of a Roman Soldier

An appended incident

And He entered into Capernaum. And a certain Centurion had a slave that was dear to him, who was sick and at the point of death. And when he heard about Jesus he sent Elders of the Jews unto Him, asking Him to come and heal his slave. And these came to Jesus and besought him earnestly, saying that the man was worthy that He should do this for him, for he loveth our nation and himself hath built the synagogue for us, and Jesus went with them. But when He was already not far from the house, the centurion sent friends, to say to Him, My Lord, take no trouble; for I am not of dignity that Thou shouldest enter beneath my roof. For this reason also I did not deem myself worthy to come to thee in person—but give direction by a word and my servant shall be healed. For I too am a man ranked under authority, having soldiers under me, and I say to one go, and he goeth, and to another come, and he cometh, and to my slave do this and he doeth it.

And when Jesus heard this He marvelled at him, and turned and said to the crowd that followed Him: **' I tell you I have not seen so great faith, not even in Israel.'**

. . . .

Now when the messenger had returned home they found the slave convalescent.

The first exemplification of the working of the new principle comes not from a Jewish but a Pagan source. The incident is striking in the extreme. He had found faith in Israel, He had found followers, but here was an unattached outsider—an officer of a foreign legion whose life—lived up to the light that was in him—is pointed out as an example to the disciples and the multitude. He had built a synagogue, in which Jesus undoubtedly preached the good news of God, later. His child-like faith in the power and kindness of Jesus was but one side of the picture. His love for his slave was the other. He considered himself of no reputation and refused to intrude.

¶ 77

The Highest Faith

Ecclesiastical cirtics have shelved this friend in a sort of spiritual *Chiltern Hundreds*. They call him a 'disciple of the gate.' But as one who loved his fellow men, the Master wrote his name large in the society of friends. The comprehensiveness of the Kingdom is epitomised and elucidated in this incident as in no other of the Gospels. Abraham Lincoln once said that if he ever found a church whose basis of fellowship was love to God and one's neighbour, he would join it. He never joined a church, but with the Roman Centurion he was a type of the Kingdon.

The Essence of Prayer

When ye pray, do not repeat the same words over again as do the Gentiles, who imagine that a multitude of words assures them a hearing. Do not imitate them. God your Father knoweth your needs before you ask them of Him.

Matthew vi. 9–13.

Our Father which art in heaven,
Hallowed be thy name,
Thy kingdom come,
Thy will be done,
As in heaven, so on the earth,
Give us this day our daily bread,
And forgive us our debts,
As we also have forgiven our debtors,
And bring us not into temptation,
But deliver us from evil.

After this manner, therefore, let your prayer be offered.

¶ 78

Reality in Prayer

In form and essence this is the pattern prayer! The introduction is a warning against mistaking a rush of words to the face for the genuine emotion of the heart. In substance He enjoins them and us not to stutter and babble and heartlessly repeat mere words over and over. It is an assurance also that prayer is not giving God information. He knows all about it.

It is very interesting to know how it contrasted with the religious standards of Judaism. It is infinitely more interesting to find out how it accords with ours. Let us analyse it.

Our Father

That means all of us. It includes the Centurion and John the Baptist, the woman taken in sin, Paul, John, the thief on the cross, Judas Iscariot, St Francis of Assissi, George Fox, and Henry the Eighth! It is all inclusive, as broad as the expanse of the heavens, as wide as the sea, as limitless as the air! Man can pre-empt the earth and the fruit thereof—he can own the cattle on a thousand hills and the hills too, but no man nor set of men can monopolise the Father. What a beautiful thought!

Which art in Heavem

Jesus taught no doctrine which modern science has discounted or set aside. The Jewish conception of heaven was based on the idea that the Earth was flat. They believed in a plurality of heavens which to them were inhabited by spirits good and evil. Of heaven Jesus spoke with great reserve. He did not define it. He did not say whether it was a place or a condition. In the model prayer He undoubtedly speaks of it as that spirit world beyond the mists of the life that now is—beyond the jar and discord of the things of sense and flesh.

Hallowed be Thy Name

The name of the supreme being had many forms. By whatever name He was called throughout the long history of Israel, the name was the most sacred on the tongue of men. The word 'Father' was not original with Jesus, but He gave it a new meaning and made reverence for it an important element in spiritual worship.

Thy Kingdon come, Thy will be done, As in heaven, so on the earth

The harmony of the world beyond is assumed. There spirits cease from striving and act in harmony, co-operation and peace here as hereafter. As popularly understood it has meant more of a devout resignation to an inevitable decree than a desire to see the will of the Highest operating in love among the children of men.

In the sense in which He uses the phrase it has a positive force and cosmic application. It is the desire which fulfils itself. The will of God frustrated by the selfishness, sloth, and greed of man. Nehemiah, like the petitioner, asks for the elimination of these 'over against his own house.' It is a prayer for the substitution of the divine for the human will in furthering the objects of the Kingdom. The object of the Kingdom is the reign of disinterested love.

¶ 79

Bread for the Body

Anti-Ebionism gives this phrase a mystical meaning. To the comfortable comforters of the breadless it could mean nothing else. How foolish it would be to ask God for that of which they have enough in store for years to come! To the vast majority of the human race it means exactly what it says. For them there is no assurance in civilisation of to-morrow's bread. In one case to pray for bread that sustains the body would be foolish, while for starving people to pray for spiritual food would be a mockery. We cannot read into the words an economic system, nor can we twist them out of their meaning in order to sustain a theological theory. He has spoken at length of the needs of the spirit. He is now linking up to the thought of God the needs of the body. The words are entirely in keeping with His thought and attitude toward the poor. The earth and the fullness thereof is the Lord's. There is enough for all. Production and distribution must be correlated. They must be of a piece with the will of God and the unity of life. It is not implied that bread will drop from the skies but that the social system shall be ethical and spiritual. If God is our Father and men our brothers, there should be no difficulty. There is, however, but it is in the practice—not in the theory. Here vain repetition are not only rewardless but blasphemy.

¶ 80

Forgiving Debts

And forgive us our debts, as we forgive our debtors
A strange comment on this phrase is the fact that the best known Christian Evangelist of modern times

is considered the best collector of bad debts in America. For that reason he is financially supported in generous manner by the Christian business men. He himself has no debts, for his business as an evangelist has made him a very rich man. His converts are the nomadic poor to whom moving is easier than payment and to whom life is a rather precarious matter of hand-to-mouth existence. When converted they pay up the bad debts of lean years, and that is a good thing. What is good business, however, may not be good Christianity. It is easy to forgive an insult or an injury that costs nothing more than a generous thought. When the forgiveness of others affects our treasury department it becomes a severe test of the spiritual nature. No limitation is appended to the request for bread. For the Father's forgiveness we make our own stipulation. 'As we have forgiven others.' To the petitioner who thinks, the condition is heart-searching, it goes to the root of things. We pray that His will be done. His will is that we forgive others. 'Bread' and 'debts' are words of vital interest in the vocabulary of the poor. There is an affinity between them that cannot be explained away. God's forgiveness means unity, harmony, and peace. We get that from Him by giving it to the measure of our ability to others.

¶ 81

Temptation

And bring us not into temptation, but deliver us from evil

The sayings of Jesus are full of antitheses—one saying set over against another to bring out the meaning by contrast and comparison. We may say of this clause as Peter said about some of the sayings of Paul. 'It is hard to understand.' But stating the difficulty is not solving the problem. God does not play with us as

a cat plays with a mouse. He knows our nature.
It is frail. But how frail or how strong it is we can only
know by temptation. Innocence may be a flabby,
innocuous thing, until it goes into the gymnasium and
has its fibre exercised and tested. If it stands the
test it becomes virtue. The gymnasium is temptation.
The paraphernalia is the desires of our lower nature.
Should we then ask to be kept from such a test? yes,
if we feel we are not equal to the strain. **If it is possible,**
Jesus prayed, **'let this cup pass from me.'** To be kept
from evil is only the other half of the antithesis, it is
another way of saying the same thing. One is the
process, the other is the result. It matters little whether
the translation be 'evil' or 'evil one,' the power that
destroys the spiritual life is the same. Half the difficulty
in understanding the passage is overcome when we
interpret it subjectively. 'Our Father, suffer us not
to be tempted to the breaking point and preserve us from
the evil that blunts the fine edge of our spiritual perceptions.' The doxology at the end of the prayer was
added in the earliest of the churches, but was not in
the original.

Review of the Pattern Prayer

This prayer is the soul at worship—breathing out
to the Father what has been learned from the great
charter. The Fatherhood of God, the brotherhood
of men, the unity of life, the basic values, the relation
to God, the relation to our neighbours, the dependence
of the individual, the conditions of peace amid world
cares. It is not a dogmatic ritual; it is a pattern, a
model. 'After this manner' is the injunction, and it
is well to keep in mind that while it embraces the fundamentals of spiritual desire it is primarily designed
for beginners. They were beginning to find difficulty
in expression, and it was only when they learned that
John the Baptist had given his disciples a form of
prayer that they requested Jesus to give them one also.

¶ 82

The A B C of Prayer

He gave them the framework, an outline, a foundation; their individual spiritual needs would suggest the details and the superstructure. In after years they would look back upon it as the first letters in the alphabet of free spiritual worship. We find no record of the use to which it was put, either while He yet was with them or after He had gone. The child mind in religion is like the child mind in the family. It asks for things; it is dimly conscious that some degree of reverence is due to the parent and the discipline of relation is something it has frequently to be reminded of. As the mind develops the relationship is assumed, and words become unnecessary. 'When I became a man,' Paul says, 'I put away childish things.' The immature mind in religion has more zeal than wisdom. The forms of speech do not keep pace with the imagination. It asks and asks amiss because the nature of the divine is but dimly revealed. As the experience trains the faculties, and communion attunes the soul, the petitioner ceases to ask the Father to set aside the laws of nature but seeks rather to know His will and do it gladly, and without hope of reward. As the soul grows, prayer changes in form. It changes its vocabulary. It communes in soliloquy, in contemplation. It begins to understand the meaning of things eternal.

The form was the point of departure. He Himself was ultimate form and substance. His life as it was lived before them was the very essence of prayer.

CHAPTER X

¶ 83

The Kingdom of God

JESUS had a name for the body of truth He taught. He called it 'the Kingdom of God.' He had a name for Himself. He called Himself 'The Son of Man.' He had a name for His followers. He called them 'friends.' I call you not servants but friends.

The Philosophy of the Spirit

With Jesus the word 'Kingdom' acquired a new meaning. The people around Him were not unfamiliar with the name. The Jews had been taught to look for a new order. It was now in their midst but there were few who had eyes to see it. Jesus was not merely a preacher. He was a teacher. His preaching was dynamic. His teaching was constructive. There are two kinds of love mentioned in the Gospels, one has a reciprocal relation—an axe to grind. The other loves the object, simply because the object is intrinsically lovely and lovable. In the Kingdom the nobler love reigned. Its object was the Father. To love the good because it is good, the truth because it is true, the beautiful because it is beautiful, is the philosophy of the spirit. The Kingdom was a spiritual society of friends. Love to God, loyalty to the Son of Man, love of the friends, loving service and self-sacrifice, were the badges of citizenship in the new Kingdom. They are the foundations of the new society. They were familiar with the commandments. He added a new one: **'A new commandment I bring to you, that ye love one another.'** This love was not to be merely a theory, it was to be tested by translation—translation into life. They were to be sons and citizens by being and doing rather than by knowing how. It was an experience, not a theory, a life not a dogma. And He Himself was the standard and test of the truth. He was the centre of the system—if it can be called a system.

His ministry began by announcing the Kingdom. It ended by sending the disciples forth to the ends of the earth to preach it. His entire ministry was occupied by illuminating, illustrating, and exemplifying it. In the Sermon on the Mount He states the fundamentals. His language was simple, His ideas were clear. When the occasion demanded it He gave an object lesson.

¶ 84

The Child as a Type of the Kingdom

He took a little child on His knee and said, **'Of such is the Kingdom of God.'** They imagined He was talking about a future state of abode. He corrects the impression: **'The Kingdom of God is within you.'** He spoke of its mysteries and explained them. He spoke of the 'keys,' and promised them to the disciples. They were unaware of it, but they had the keys already in their possession. There were conditions. For the rich to enter was hard—very hard. For the poor it was easy—very easy. It was to be received as a little child. It was to be a unity—not a uniformity. **'A Kingdom divided,'** He pointed out, was a Kingdom tumbling to ruins. His was to be held intact by spiritual power. **'That they may be one, Father,'** He prayed. When He sent the disciples forth it was to preach the Kingdom.

¶ 85

Conduct and Character

Citizenship in the Kingdom was based on love, Love to God and Man. It had no social limitations. It was universal. He enumerates types of citizens, the poor, the humble, the pure in heart, the kind. Current types of piety were legalistic. They prayed and worshipped and gave alms to be seen of men. With the new it was to be different. Whatever they did was to be done quietly, unostentatiously as unto the Father and not unto men. In the old times, seasons, feasts, fasts, phlacteries counted. In the new, character and conduct as the outworking of love, were the signs of citizenship.

¶ 86

The Distinctive Feature

The world was full of needy people. Men were self-centred and imagined they were doing well if they fulfilled the naked requirements of the law. Loving service, was the distinctive feature of the Kingdom. Love did not ask how little, but how much it could do. He Himself came not to be ministered unto but to minister. He told them to give until they had nothing left, to lend and not expect to be repaid, to return good for evil, and a kind word for an insult.

¶ 87

The Joyful Heart

People were sin-stricken and soul-weary. The message of the Kingdom was the good news of God. God's good news was God's love, and it gave peace to the troubled, and hope to the sinner. The channels through which it flowed were human hearts. One joyful heart gave another joy, and the love stream broadened and deepened.

¶ 88

No Class Distinctions

Class consciousness and class distinctions—then as now—were a curse. In the Kingdom men were sons, and equally sons. They might be different in a thousand ways but in this they were equally alike—they were members of the same family and owed loyalty and allegiance to one common Father. All differences were fused into the elembic of love. If special consideration was shown to any, it was to those most in need of it. The healing power of love was the peculiar privilege of the sick, the sinner, the poor, and the sorrowful.

¶ 89

Contempt for the World

'Extreme contempt for the world'—worldy goods—worldly honours, standards, and opinions, was one of the Kingdom's most pronounced characteristics.

The earliest conflict in the Master's life was with the men who considered that a Man's life consisted in what he owned. Jesus denied it, and taught His disciples to deny it. When a rich man came He offered a choice between the Kingdom and the world, between wealth of the heart and wealth that perished. If he couldn't let go, he couldn't come in. If a wise man came he was told that he would have to be re-born before he could enter the fellowship of the poor, the humble, and the simple-hearted. Not many wise men, not many rich men came.

The Kingdom was an uncongenial atmosphere for men whose god was either stomach or brain.

¶ 90

Love and Law

In religion men were playing with shadows. They were punctilious censorians and severe. They observed the forms, performed lip service, and talked in pious phrases. The cardinal canon in the intricate system was the Sabbath. It was originally intended as a day of rest from labour. In the time of Jesus it was observed chiefly by the men who, considering labour beneath their dignity, nothing in that respect to rest from! When they saw Jesus heal on the Sabbath they accused Him of violating the law. According to them, when He plucked the ears of corn He was performing work. His answers are always to the point. Over against every foolish insistence of the old régime He puts the spiritual standards of the new. In the Kingdom service to man, to one another knows no limitations. 'The Sabbath was made for man, not man for the Sabbath.'

¶ 91

As a Little Child

Despite His explanations the Kingdom was not clearly understood. A little boy is brought to Jesus by his father. The boy is distraught and is foaming at the mouth. Current belief said he was possessed of a demon. Jesus took the little fellow in His arms and he became calm and quiet and rational. The disciples were astonished. 'Why could we not do that?' they asked. **'You can by prayer and fasting,'** He said. Then Jesus and the boy and his father and the disciples in twos and threes walked down the road to Capernaum.

¶ 92

Bickering about Rank

When they entered the house of Jesus and sat down there was a silent pause. **'Tell me,'** Jesus said, as He looked at the disciples, **'what were you talking about as you came along the road?'** The words were graciously and tenderly spoken, but they cut into the conscience with convincing force. Some one at last spoke: 'We were arguing about which of us should be the greatest in the Kingdom.' He had taught them to tarry for its coming. He had outlined its basic values and principles. Now He had exemplified its working in loving service, but instead of conferring with each other as how they could follow His example, they were bickering about rank.

Later they returned to the selfish aspect and asked: 'Who is greatest in the Kingdom?' He took a little child and setting him in the midst said: **'Except ye be converted from this selfish point of view and become as this little child you cannot even enter the Kingdom.'**

¶ 93

How to attain Greatness

Salomi came to Him and presented the claims of her sons, John and James, to pre-eminence in the Kingdom. She thought one of them had a right to sit on His right hand and the other on His left. Whether she had in her mind a political Kingdom or a future state is not quite clear, but there is nothing obscure in His answer. John and James were evidently standing there beside their mother. Jesus directed His answer not to Salomi but to them: **'Are ye able to drink of the same cup, and be baptized with the same baptism as shall be given to me?'**

They answered 'Yes.' He told them He knew they were but as for the coveted places they were

not His to give but the Father's. The others were
angry at John and James, but Jesus smoothed over
the ruffled feelings by again explaining that among
the Gentiles princes and rulers exercised authority,
but in the Kingdom the badge of greatness was
service. **'Whosoever will be great among you, let
him be your minister, and whosoever will be chief
let him be your servant.'**
They might not have clearly understood this at
the time, but there could have been no more doubt
when He illustrated it on another occasion by girding
Himself with a towel and washing their feet.

¶ 94

Dignities, Titles, Distinctions

In the Kingdom, the pregnancy of love covered all
the affairs of men. Its religion and ethics were so inter-
woven that they could not be separated. Kindness is
greater than wisdom and a loving heart is of more importance than a brilliant mind. The mysterious gulf
that divides the human from the divine is bridged. He
is the bridge. Force of arms, either of patriots or angels
is foreign to it. It has no slaves, no vested material
interests, no spoils of office, or external rewards. The
world was to be leavened with love—the will of God was
the ruling principle and the dominating force. Dignities,
titles, distinctions were out of place. He was the Master,
and the members were all brethren. The harlot with a
thirst for righteousness was of more concern to Him
than the self-righteous Scribe or Pharisee. He pictured
harlots and publicans marching into the Kingdom while
the punctilious and self-centred religious leaders remained outside.

¶ 95

Theory and Practice in Religion

There were times when He stated the basic values of

religion in a single sentence. If any doubt remained He would illustrate it with a story. Over a thousand years before Jesus, the Jew had been taught to love his neighbour as himself. In that case the neighbour was also a Jew. He reminded a critic of this one day, and the critic asked: 'Who is my neighbour?' The answer of Jesus gives the difference between the theory of the old and the practice of the new. He did not deal in glittering genialities. He told a parable that left nothing unsaid, even to the dullest of minds. One day, on the road to Jericho, a Jew fell among thieves. They robbed and beat him, and left him on the roadside, nigh unto death. A priest came by on his way to worship, saw the man, and passed on. A levite, another kind of priest, came by, looked at the man, and went on his way. The dying man had a claim on these men. They were the representatives of God. Then a Samaritan came along, saw the Jew in his plight, put soothing oil on his wounds, bandaged them up, and put him on his own (the Samaritan's) beast, and took him to an inn. There he stayed all night with him and when he left next day, he told the innkeeper to give the man all he needed, and charge the bill to him. **'Which of these men was neighbour to the man who fell amongst the thieves,'** Jesus asked. There was no way but the right way out for the critic; he confessed that the pagan was the better Jew. In such manner Jesus broke down race barriers and distinctions, and taught the principles of the Kingdom.

¶ 96

The Essence of Religion

The contempt of the orthodox religionist for the sinner and the unlearned, was equalled only by his contempt for the foreigner—for the outsider. There are passages which would seem to interpret Jesus as partaking of this contempt. They are like false notes in music. They do not harmonise with the tone and tenor of the great charter or with the universal outlook which characterises His teachings. He held up a Roman soldier as the greatest example of faith. He points to a Samaritan as the greatest example of Philanthropy. To a Samaritan woman He defined the essence of the Kingdom. One day He was sitting beside a well within half an hour's journey from Shechem. On one side was Mount Ebal, and on the other Gerizim. This was the home, and these were the sacred mountains of the Samaritans whose bread was to the Jews as the flesh of swine. A Samaritan woman came to draw water, and He asked her for a drink. The woman was astonished that a Jew should break the age-long antipathy by accepting a favour from a woman of a race they despised. By the kind tone, the gentle look, the noble bearing, she knew He was a prophet, and she asked Him to explain. He told her of the water she knew not of —of living water that refreshed the soul. He spoke of the well, and its blessing, and of the sacredness of the mountains where her fathers worshipped. 'And yet,' she said, 'You tell us that it is only at Jerusalem that men should worship.'

Jesus said: **'Woman, believe me, the hour cometh when ye shall neither in this mountain nor yet at Jerusalem, worship the Father. But the hour cometh and now is when the true worshippers shall worship the Father in spirit and in truth.'**

And they who worship the Father in spirit and in truth shall know the truth, and the truth shall make them free, and the free spirit in worship discovers the Father's will and in love makes it His own. That, Jesus says, is the essence of the Kingdom.

¶ 97

Institutions of the Kingdom

Of canonical law or a system of applied morality

or of creeds or liturgies, there is no trace in the teaching of Jesus. He was baptized by John, but He does not seem to have insisted upon it with others—not even His disciples. His baptism was of fire and spirit. The breaking of bread and the drinking of wine, were pointed out as symbols of His life and death. By these they would remember Him and follow in His footsteps. The observance required no priest. He Himself was the bread from heaven. The citizen of the Kingdom was a priest. The repasts of the Master and His friends were the most sacred, joyful, and enjoyable moments of their lives. They were communions in a real sense. In this heart to heart fellowship the world receded, the body was a matter of secondary importance. They were at one because love predominated and sharply contrasted personalities became fused and blended in a common atmosphere of exultation and idealism. He quoted from the prophets, whose idealism was the heritage of His people, but the idea of a sacred book or books containing infallible codes of conduct, was foreign to His idea of the Kingdom.

¶ 98

The Kingdom and the Church

In the first three evangelists, the word Kingdom occurs over one hundred times. In the fourth evangelist it occurs four times. In all other books of the New Testament the word occurs only about twenty-five times. He used the word 'church' (*Ecclesia*—Assembly) twice. Matthew alone records the reference. Despite the doubtful meaning attached to the word 'church' it occurs over one hundred times, in the later writings of the New Testament. The prominence given to the 'Kingdom' by Jesus was transferred to the 'church' by His followers. Why this transfer of emphasis? Was it because the Jewish mind could not fully comprehend that it was spiritual and not

material, universal and not national? The Roman
eagles still flew over the Holy City. The Jewish hierarchy was still intact and unmoved. Despite His
miracles and parables the bulk of the people still clung
to the old régime.

Were the New Testament writers timid about using
the words 'king' or 'Kingdom' lest the use would give
offence to Cæsar? The apostles were charged with
violating a decree of Cæsar and teaching 'that there
is another King—one Jesus.'

¶ 99

A Misunderstanding

We have some records of apocalyptic sayings and
prediction of Jesus that were not fulfilled. That He
was misunderstood is beyond question. His teaching
was bound to come into juxtaposition with current
religious beliefs. As it did so it was modified. There
is no evidence that He changed His conception, but
there is abundant proof that to the last, despite the
wonderful illumination of the parables, His followers
did not fully understand that to Him the rule of God
in the heart, the motive power of love, the will of God
as a rule of faith and conduct was the essence of the
Kingdom. It was after His resurrection that they
asked, 'Lord, wilt Thou at this time restore the Kingdom
to Israel?'

In the earliest record of the church at Jerusalem
we see the beginning of the change in which the Kingdom recedes and the church evolves. The first Christian Community surpassed the most orthodox Jews
in the punctilious observances and usages of Judaism.
They conceived the religion of Jesus as the peculiar and
exclusive property of Israel. The Gentiles might enter
the church, but they would have to enter Judaism first
by the gateway of circumcision. It was Paul the converted Pharisee, who became the champion of the free

spirit and demanded the right of Gentiles to membership without circumcision. He had a clearer vision of the Kingdom than any of his contemporaries, and he prevailed. The Jewish Christians, however, continued their existence within the pale of the Jewish economy. Peter was accused by the Christian church at Jerusalem, just as Jesus was accused by the Pharisees—of eating with sinners (Gentile converts). In self-defence, Peter related that in a vision God had revealed to him that what what he had made clean no man could make unclean. When they heard of the vision they said in astonishment: 'Then hath God also to the Gentiles granted repentance unto life.' In the light of this controversy over Jews and Gentiles, circumcision and non-circumcision we see more clearly why Jesus Himself was involved by the evangelists who quote Him as pronouncing a curse upon whomsoever failed to fulfil the most minute requirement of the law. But how He could do this and at the same time castigate with withering scorn the religious hypocrite who scrupulously observed the rubbish while they neglected the real values of life, is difficult to understand

¶ 100

The Kingdom Ignored

The earliest Christian took over the synagogue. In the course of time, some centuries later, the temple, priesthood, vestments, holy days, ritual, and genuflexions, were, as far as possible, incorporated into the new society. The Sabbath, baptism, and the Lord's supper lost their original simplicity and became subjects of speculation and heated controversy. His birth, life, and death, and the things He taught, congealed into dogmas, creeds, and codes over which Christians hated, fought, and killed each other. As these things became prominent the idea of the Kingdom became indefinitive, hazy, and obscure. It never regained its place

¶ 101

What the Kingdom is not

The creeds of Christendom ignore it. The church throughout all ages ignored it. Perversions of it have arisen. One sect claims the keys of heaven and declares itself the Kingdom. Another claims itself the Kingdom on the basis of an infallible book, another on the basis of an infallible church or faith, or ministry. To others it is a future fulfilment of an apocalyptic dream; to still others, it is a second coming of the Messiah. Each of these may have done good service by the preservation of certain aspects of truth, but the Kingdom is none of these. It is not the church at Jerusalem, nor yet at Antioch. It is not the church of the fathers, nor the medieval church, nor the church of the twentieth century.

¶ 102

The Spirit of the Kingdom

It is the active operation of invisible spiritual laws in the hearts of men. It is an inward force with inevitable outward manifestations. It is the vehicle through which divine life flows into the relations of society and the instrument by which the life finds expression. It is the wheat amongst the tares, the good seed in the good ground, and the yeast preserving, and expanding the bread. In the ages when the church was corrupt it preserved it, when it was dead it resurrected it.

¶ 103

The Kingdom the Custodian of the Faith

In the present age when the church is as the Jewish Church was in the time of Augustus, it is the Kingdom that keeps the religion of Jesus alive and vital in the lives of men. The church is a means to an end, the end is the Kingdom. Creeds, rituals, sacred books, holy days, and all the infinite variety of auxiliaires are subservient to the purpose for which they exist —that purpose is to advance the Kingdom. When a church appoints itself supreme gatekeeper of the Kingdom, it is no longer Christian. When it fails to recognise other sheep of the same fold, it has discarded the comprehensiveness of the love of the Master for the exclusive and poisonous leaven of the Pharisees.

¶ 104

The Supreme Test

The final tests of all sects, all auxiliaries, all religious movement is: Do they promote the Kingdom? Do they sweeten human life, do they raise it into higher moral standards, do they increase mutual confidence and love and esteem, do they kindle hearts with loyalty to Him? If they do, they are instruments of the Kingdom! If they do not, they belong to the diocese of Laodicea, the communicants of which God spewed out of His mouth.

The need of the world, and the failure of religious organisations to meet that need is driving thoughtful men toward the ideal of the Kingdom as Jesus preached it. Only when that ideal receives the prominence He gave it, can we hope for a united and progressive movement toward a world-wide spiritual revival. Only then can we have an answer to His prayer for the unity of believers and the regnancy of love in the hearts of men.

THE KINGDOM ILLUMINATED

The Parables

¶ 105

Foreword

In Archbishop Trench's book on the parables (probably the most widely circulated and least read book ever written on the subject), we are warned that: 'The parables may not be made primary sources of doctrine. Doctrine otherwise and already established may be illustrated or indeed further confirmed by them, but it is not allowable to constitute doctrine first by their aid. They may be the outer ornamental fringe, but not the main texture of the proof.'

¶ 106

Light and the Kingdom

Perhaps the good bishop would not object if we made them the 'primary source' of light! To him the doctrines were all established and 'confirmed.' The last word had been said, and the feet laid down so heavily on the confirmation had turned to bronze. The 'ornamental fringe' to the modern seeker after light is not the parables but the entire fabric of theological controversy which has obscured the light of the Kingdom. And the 'main texture' is not what a bishop thinks or the fathers wrote or the 'established' doctrines of warring sects, but what He taught and did.

In the Sermon on the Mount, we have the antitheses.

In the parables we have parallelism. The former is direct, the latter is a word picture of life and nature which provokes the mind to find the implied but hidden meaning. A story is told, the meaning of which is obvious, but as the narrative proceeds, the mind of the listener is on the alert to discover the implied parallel, the story within the story. In the hands of Jesus the parable received a new value. It became a new method of teaching. It had been used before but never to such a lofty purpose or on so large a scale.

¶ 107

Word Pictures

The reason for the adoption of the parable as a

means of conveying truth, is not hard to find. Comparatively few people in the crowds following Him had the capacity for sustained attention, and those who had were tasters, sniffing for heresy or trouble. Even His disciples were not overladen with it. **'If the blind lead the blind,'** He said, **'both shall fall into the ditch.'** Here is a word picture which would be obvious to a child. Yet it was not clear to Simon Peter, and he said: 'Explain to us this parable.' The answer gives us a clue to the purpose of the new vehicle: **'Are you also without understanding?'** Jesus asked.

It was best adopted to the mass mind. It gave the maximum of instruction with a minimum of offence. The Pharisees would look upon the parables as the 'outer ornamental fringe.' They would find them difficult to assail. On the other hand the dullest mind could remember a story. They were all such stories as the hearers would repeat at home and discuss in the market place, and both parables—the obvious and the less obvious—were essential to complete understanding.

The parable was head of a large family, every member of which, allegory, metaphor, maxim, proverb, similitude, and paradox, Jesus constantly used with force and originality. While primarily for the child mind of the grown-up people, the parables are incomparable as literature, and as such shed more light on the spiritual laws of the Kingdom than all the commentaries that have been issued in nineteen centuries.

¶ 108

What is taught by Parables

Matthew is the evangelist of the Kingdom, Luke is the democratic illuminator of the love of God toward all mankind. Mark is the succinct chronicler of events, and few of the parables find a place in his chronicle. John has a number of sayings which belong to the parable

family, but none of them take the story form. In the
fourth Gospel, Jesus speaks of Himself as the Door of
the Sheep, the Good Shepherd, the Vine and the Light
of the World. They are allegories rather than parables.
The parables are incorporated here because primarily
they illuminate the mind of the Master. For that
reason we are not particularly concerned with chronology,
nor will we, except incidentally, analyse the variant forms.
The parables will be considered in four groups. The first
group illustrates the law of love as it affects the individual
in the conditions and environments of the Kingdom.
The second group throws light on the law of love as it
comes in contact with Pharisaism. The course of the
Kingdom, its law of growth as illustrated in the third
and fourth is concerned with responsibility and judgment.

¶ 109

The Law of Love and the Individual

**'A certain lender had two debtors: the one
owed five hundred pence, and the other fifty,
when they had not wherewith to pay, he forgave
them both. Which of them therefore will love
him most?'**
Simon answered and said, He, I suppose, to whom
he forgave the most. And He said unto him, **'Thou
hast rightly judged.'**

Luke vii. 41–43.

The scene of this parable is the house of Simon the
Pharisee. The occasion is an unusual incident. He
had accepted the invitation of the Pharisee to dine
with him. As they sat at the meal a woman of the
street entered, and gave vent to her emotions. She
had heard Him somewhere, and a struggle between
that which was low and that which was high in her
nature had ensued. It was the overwhelming sense
of gratitude that urged her to act. A burden had

rolled away — her heart had become tender, and brushing aside all conventionality and reserve, she entered the house of Simon as an unwelcome intruder. There, forgetful of everything else, she emotionally exploded before Him; her hot tears falling on His feet, she wiped them with her hair, and annointed Him with ointment. To the average person the scene would have been pathetic and moving in the extreme. Simon with difficulty restrained his indignation. He said nothing, but his mind was seething. Jesus saw it on his face, every line and furrow became vocal. **'Simon,'** said Jesus, **'I have something to say to you,'** and the Pharisee politely replied, 'Master, say on.' Then He told the parable of the debtors. There is something daring in this picture. Only Jesus could imagine a Shylock foregoing his pound of flesh! For He alone could see that goodness was fundamental, and evil incidental! We have what seems to be an inherent distrust in our fellow beings, and our eyes and ears are ever on the alert for the worst aspects of the lives of others. Simon mused within himself: 'If this man is a prophet he would know that this creature is a fallen woman!' Yes, He did know, and He knew Simon too, and He weighed them in the scales of the Kingdom and the orthodox devotee of the temple was the lighter of the two.

He was not inconsiderate of His host either. As a teacher He let the lesson do its work. He asked Simon to decide frankly which of the two debtors loved most. Simon told Him he supposed it was the one to whom most had been forgiven.

'I came as your guest,' Jesus said, **'and you gave me no water to wash my feet. You gave me no kiss of salutation, yet in the courtesies for which as a leader you take credit to yourself, you have been put to shame by an abandoned woman.'**

There is no answer, no defence, no apology. As the woman stands there, Jesus tells Simon that her sins are forgiven and why. She loved much. He finally, amid the mutterings of the guests, turned to the woman and told her that her faith had saved her, and she could go away in peace.

This is the type of spiritual value that has never been formulated into a dogma. That the tears of the harlot are more acceptable to God than the complacent negative goodness of a Pharisee of ancient or modern times, is a hard lesson to learn, and few there are that learn it.

¶ 110

The Measure of Forgiveness

'The Kingdom of heaven is likened unto a certain king, which would make a reckoning with his servants. And when he had begun to reckon, one was brought unto him, which owed him ten thousand talents. But forasmuch as he had not wherewith to pay his lord commanded him to be sold, and his wife and children, and all that he had, and payment to be made. The servant therefore fell down and worshipped him saying, Lord have patience with me and I will pay thee all. And the lord of that servant, being moved with compassion, released him and forgave him the debt. But that servant went out and found one of his fellow-servants, which owed him a hundred pence, and he laid hold on him, and took him by the throat, saying, Pay thou what thou owest. So his fellow servant fell down and besought him, saying, Have patience with me and I will pay thee. And he would not, but went and cast him into prison, till he should pay his due. So when his fellow servants saw what was done they were exceedingly sorry, and came and told their lord all that was done. Then his lord called him unto him and saith to him, Thou wicked servant, I forgave thee all that debt because thou besoughtest me. Shouldst thou not

have mercy on thy fellow servant even as I had mercy on thee? And his lord was wroth and delivered him to the tormentors till he should pay all that was due.

Even so shall your heavenly Father do unto you if ye forgive not every one his brother from your hearts.'

Matthew xviii. 23–35.

Jesus had just finished telling the disciples how members of the Kingdom should treat a brother who had trespassed against another. The offended one was to see the erring brother personally and point out the offence. If he was amenable to reason he was gained, and there was an end of it. If not, the offended was to take two or three others, and repeat the visit. If he remained obdurate he was to be taken before the assembly. If he would not abide by the decision of the assembly he was to be cast out as a heathen. Then Peter asks: 'How often shall my brother sin against me and I forgive him: till seven times?' Peter probably imagined this a generous measure of forgiveness. He must have looked aghast when Jesus said,—'**Not seven times, but seventy times seven.**' Those to whom religion is a respectable habit of mind, are as dumbfounded as Peter was. No religious sect pays any attention either to the method or measure of these injunctions. They are unthinkable to the average man either in or out of organised religion.

They gaze at Him open-mouthed. It is utterly beyond their range. In order to bring it down to their understanding, He tells the story of the unmerciful debtor. The King in the story is taking stock. He discovers one man who owes him ten thousand talents —a fabulous sum. He determines to exact the last penny. The servant prostrates himself, and pleads for time. The King relents and forgives him all.

Then the servant goes out and meets another servant who owes him a hundred pence, seizes him by the throat and demands the money. The debtor pleads, but pleads in vain. He is thrust into prison. The King hears of it and summoning the unmerciful man, executes the original judgment. The hidden meaning — which is quite plain — is that the unmerciful servant is the man who has been forgiven much but is not willing to forgive even in an infinitesimal degree his brother. Jesus says: **'Even so (as the King) shall my heavenly Father do unto you, if ye forgive not every one his brother from your hearts.'** He told this to Peter and the twelve and to all their spiritual descendants, and if God executes the Judgment as King in the parable did there will be no congestion of population in heaven. Membership in the Kingdom of Heaven presupposes a heart full of love and human kindness. To such a heart all things are possible. The harlot had it and Simon had not. It is found in places where we least expect it, but wherever it is found, there is God and His Kingdom.

¶ III

The Religion of a Heretic

'A certain man was going down from Jerusalem to Jericho; and he fell among robbers, which both stripped him and beat him, and departed, leaving him half dead.

And by chance a certain priest was going down that way: and when he saw him, he passed by on the other side.

And in a like manner a Levite also when he came to the place, and saw him, passed by on the other side.

But a certain Samaritan as he journeyed, came where he was: and when he saw him, he was moved with compassion, and came to him, and bound up his wounds, pouring on them oil and wine: and he set him on his own beast, and brought him to an inn, and took care of him.

And on the morrow he took out twopence, and gave them to the host, and said, Take care of him: and whatsoever thou spendeth more, I, when I come back again, will repay thee.'
Luke x. 30–35 (R.V.).

The story of the Samaritan was told to illustrate the sum total of all religion—Love to God and love to one's neighbour. A lawyer, in quest of an argument, asks Jesus what he shall do to inherit eternal life. Jesus forces him back on his own standard of conduct: **'What is written in the law?'** The lawyer knows and answers: 'To love God and my neighbour.' Jesus replied: **'Thou hast answered right—this do and thou shalt live.'** The lawyer asks the eternal question: 'Who is my neighbour?' We can talk for days and weeks about abstractions without uncovering our meanness. A neighbour is a concrete entity, and the moment we enter the discussion we are confronted with responsibility. Jesus did not embarrass the lawyer by a personal reply. The question had a universal interest. He gave an impersonal and universal answer. He expounded the law of the Kingdom as it related to neighbourship.

A Jew on the road between Jerusalem and Jericho was robbed and beaten by some Jewish thieves. When they had deprived him of his property, and beaten him into helplessness, they left him lying on the roadside. A priest came along, saw the man at the point of death, but did not offer help. He was probably on his way to the temple. Anyway, whatever excuse he offered to himself seems to have been satisfactory. He passed on. He was followed by a Levite—another kind of priest. He also seems to have had a pressing engagement, for he too passed on. No explanation to the lawyer was necessary about these busy men. He knew it was their peculiar professional business to render aid in a case of this sort. Their brutal neglect was the veiled parallel to the thread of the story. They refused to a brother what the law demanded they should give to beasts—

merciful help in time of pain and distress or need.
Mercy was a weighty matter of the law.   It was his
function to teach that and to urge its exercise.   No
one was looking, however, and with a faith in God as
slim as faith in his brother, he hurried on.

Then came a Samaritan, who, to the Jew, was a
heretic, and a foreigner.   He saw the dying Jew on the
roadside, and dismounting from his beast began to
minister to his needs.   He poured oil on the wounds,
bandaged them up, comforting him while he was doing it.
He put him on the beast, and walking beside him conveyed him to an inn, where he stayed all night with him.
When he left next day, he gave the landlord instructions
to care for the sufferer and charge the bill to his account.

**'Which now, of these three, thinketh thou, was
the neighbour unto him that fell among thieves?'**
Jesus asked, as He finished the parable.   There was but
one answer, 'He that showed mercy on him.'   And the
incident ends by Him saying: **'Go and do thou
likewise.'**   Here, then, we have the religion of a
heretic from Gerizim weighed in the balance with the
religion of an orthodox priest from Mount Zion, and
He lets the critic pronounce judgment!   And when
pronounced it was the Law of the Kingdom, and
the warp and woof of the religion of Jesus.

And the judgment stands and stands for ever.   'Am
I my brother's keeper?' asks the heretic of Gerizim!
Can disinterested love open the door of the Kingdom?
Ask the Centurion of Capernaum!   Can the tears of a
penitent harlot outweigh the religion of a hardened
ecclesiastical leader?   Ask the street walker of Capernaum!   These are the people who become His friends.

¶ 112

A Good Investment

**The Kingdom of heaven is like unto a treasure
hidden in the field; which a man found, and hid:**

and in his joy he goeth and selleth all that he hath and buyeth that field.

Matthew xiii. 44.

We can find apt analogies for most of His word pictures of divine truth, but the treasure hid in the field belongs exclusively to the orient. The best analogy in modern life is the man who discovers oil, and forthwith exerts every effort to get possession of the land. So much romance and adventure has been associated with such discoveries, that the phrase 'struck oil' has become a common one, in those parts of the world where such discoveries have changed men in a day from penury to opulence.

Whatever way one looks at the picture, it has the same meaning to our western minds. It was a good investment. So is the Kingdom, of course, but men are not parting with much in order to possess it. They are taking no chances in matters economic to possess themselves of spiritual wealth.

In the parable of the hidden treasure Jesus takes an illustration of common experience in the East, where a man often buried his most valued treasure in a hole in the ground. Occasionally he died and carried the secret away with him. Later, when some one discovered it, the finder would at once proceed to part with all he had, in order to possess the field containing the treasure. He is not teaching economics or political economy. The emphasis must be put where it belongs—on the parallel truth. When a man discovers in the law of the Kingdom the secret of living, he proceeds to possess it by getting rid of the things that stand in the way. Greed and covetousness and all the kindred brood of vices that poison the spiritual life, must give way before love. The man who discovers the real thing becomes enthusiastic, he has an inward joy that makes itself felt in his relations with others. The man who strikes oil in the Kingdom discovers the oil of joy.

That is the essence of the parable.

The twin parable of the pearl of great price, is a companion picture. There is nothing particularly meritorious in a pearl merchant selling all he had in order to secure the pearl of great price. It was good business. He was after profit. The inference to be drawn is that if a man could own the earth, and lose his life, he would be nothing profited. **'This is what a man does in business.'** Jesus is telling them. So it is in the Kingdom. The profits are spiritual—joy of spirit, satisfaction of heart, peace of conscience. To get possession of these it becomes necessary to give up the questionable pleasure of either mind or body. From the viewpoint of the Kingdom, it is good business.

CHAPTER XI

¶ 113

The Ethics of Importunity

'Which of you shall have a friend, and shall go unto him at midnight, and say unto him, Friend, lend me three loaves, for a friend of mine is come to me from a journey, and I have nothing to set before him.

And he from within shall answer and say, Trouble me not: the door is now shut, and my children are now with me in bed: I cannot rise and give thee.

I say unto you, though he will not rise and give him because he is his friend, yet because of his importunity he will arise and give him as many as he needeth.'

Luke xi. 5–8.

WE cannot imagine Jesus advising a man, that if he does not receive what he asks for at the first asking, to keep on nagging until he gets it! Ethically that is a questionable procedure. An Eastern merchant often asks twice as much as an article is worth, with the expectation that the buyer will haggle and argue until the merchant making a series of concessions arrives at the real price. The procedure is common in the East. Overcharging is as common with us, but we have no time for haggling, so we pay.

While the story is less obvious to us than to the oriental mind, the parallel is quite plain.

A Spiritual Voyage of Discovery

He had just been teaching them the model prayer. Now He gives them some ideas concerning the spirit of it. He tells the story of the friend at midnight to illustrate one phrase—persistence. If an ungracious neighbour grudgingly grants a request in an exigency, how much more willing will the Father grant the request of His children. They will learn how to pray by praying. The request for daily bread goes hand in hand with the desire that the will of God be done. They will make mistakes, but they are not to be discouraged. Importunity is not nagging, with them. It is a spiritual voyage of discovery. They have chart and compass, but they are merely guides to show the way. Explorers need courage to reach the goal. So does the citizen of the Kingdom. There are times when the violation of a spiritual law is as helpful as its observance. We ask for things and get them, only to discover that we have asked for something which becomes a curse   Importunity in prayer is not the mere repetition of a request. It is learning what to pray for. It is the blending in purpose of our spirits with the spirit of God. It is keeping at it until we know that the blending is complete.

The lesson of importunity is for children in the faith. It is for the beginner. The spiritual nature asks for little, needs little. The beginner who is unconscious that he is asking God to set aside the laws of the universe, must learn sense and proportion by carrying on. To cease, is to cut the nerve of aspiration. The parable is the story of Jacob wrestling with the angel, adopted for the use of the children of the Kingdom.

The will to believe brought them into the Kingdom. The will to materialise, to make real their dreams becomes evidence of citizenship. Knock and it shall be opened, ask and ye shall receive, keep on knocking and asking— carry on!

¶ 114

A Woman and the Law

'There was in a city a judge, which feared not God, and regardeth not man:

And there was a widow in that city: and she came oft unto him saying, Avenge me of mine adversary.

And he would not for a while:

But afterwards he said within himself, Though I fear not God nor regard man: yet because this widow troubleth me, I will avenge her, lest she wear me out by her continual coming.'

Luke xviii, 2-5.

The story of the ungracious friend and the story of the unjust judge are companion parables. They have a similar motive and teach the same truth. Here again let us observe that He is not teaching jurisprudence. He is telling a story to fix in the mind a principle. The Kingdom of Heaven suffered violence and the violent take it by storm. In this case it is a woman who persists. She is a widow, who has been illegally deprived of her rights. She takes the legal course to regain them. The judge hears her case but strings her along from day to day without applying the law. She is a widow and her existence depends upon her rights. Jesus describes the Judge as a man who neither reverenced God nor regarded man—and woman less than either. The woman finding the Judge obdurate and lazy, uses the only weapon at her disposal—her tongue. She uses it, as woman has had to do in all ages. She uses it with increasing force until the old man said within :himself 'I can defy God and man with measurable success, but this woman will wear me out with continual coming!' So he avenges her, not because she was right, but because she gave him no rest until he had done his duty, and applied the law. The contrasts are, an unjust judge and a loving Father; a persistent woman, knowing she was right, and the child of the Kingdom with hope deferred. If this Judge yielded to importunity, will not your Father hear your prayers offered day and night? He spent whole nights in prayer Himself. Prayer is not a matter of duration, nor place, nor posture, but its mysteries are only revealed to those who will do what is necessary for effectual communion, and one of the essentials is continual exercise.

¶ 115

The Mind of a Capitalist

'The ground of a certain rich man brought forth plentifully: and he reasoned with himself, saying, What shall I do, because I have not where to bestow my fruits? And he said, This will I do. I will pull down my barns and build greater; and there will I bestow all my corn and my goods. And I will say to my soul, Soul, thou hast much goods laid up for many years; take thine ease, eat, drink, and be merry. But God said unto him, Thou foolish one, this night thy soul is required of thee; and the things which thou hast prepared, whose shall they be? So is he that layeth up treasure for himself and is not rich toward God.'

Luke xii. 16–21 (R.V.).

The parable of the rich fool is as obvious as the parable of the unjust steward is obscure. We can easily comprehend the methods by which a crooked steward would provide for emergencies by carrying favour with his master's tenants, but when Jesus tells His disciples to make friends of the mammon of unrighteousness, nobody knows what He means. Many have told us what they think it means, but their interpretations have only added chaos to confusion. The wires have been crossed at some point and the message has suffered in transmission.

Immediately following the injunction is one of the most characteristic and clear cut of all His teachings: **'Ye cannot serve God and Mammon.'** That is the law of the Kingdom. Not a whit less clear is this story of the barren-hearted capitalist. He uses the brutal language of the vulgar rich: 'Eat, drink, and be merry.' His crops are good, his success is phenomenal. 'I will pull down my barns and build greater,' he muses. Then when his produce is stored he will tell his soul to take its ease—'for many years.' There is much poverty that spells misery, but there is no misery of want so miserable as the overglutted satisfaction of wealth.

The rich fool is a type not unfamiliar to any age. In modern life he adds to his soul's satisfaction a respectable denomination and an ultra-respectable party. He is the patron of charities, an habitue of exclusive clubs, and talks, as if he were going to live for ever. He creates nothing, he earns nothing, he lives by the sweat of the other faces, his opulence is at the expense of another's penury, his ease is secured by another's pain. He is protected by law, coddled by religion, and fawned upon by the truculent. Yet when his hour comes these cannot hold him. He must go. The death angel lays his hand on him and his grip relaxes. 'Thou fool! this night thy soul is required of thee, then what becomes of the barns and wealth? so is every one that layeth up treasure for himself and is not rich toward God!'

¶ 116

Self Measurement

'Two men went up into the temple to pray; one was a Pharisee, and the other a publican. The Pharisee stood and prayed thus to himself, God, I thank thee that I am not as the rest of men, extortioners, unjust, adulterers, or even as

**this publican. I fast twice in the week; I give
tithes of all that I get. But the publican, standing afar off, would not lift so much as his eyes
unto heaven, but he smote his breast saying,
God, be merciful to me, a sinner.'**
Luke xviii. 10–13 (R.V.).

By a modern Jewish critic this parable has been
called a caricature of a Pharisee. Perhaps it is. Shylock
was also a caricature. Both pictures have been objected
to by the Jews. They might just as easily have been
Englishmen or Frenchmen or Americans. It is of no
consequence whether the words were thought or uttered.
Jesus paints a word picture of the mind. That such
minds exist is only too obvious.

No Jew will deny that the typical Pharisee was
capable of thinking such self-righteous thoughts. For
the most grotesque caricature of the Pharisees we do
not search Christian literature, but Jewish. The
talmud speaks of them as a 'plague.' They were
catalogued under many heads. The 'shoulder'—Pharisee was the type whose shoulders were bowed down by
the weight of his own good deeds. The 'borrower—
Pharisee' begged the loan of a little time that he might
perform an extra good work. The 'calculating—
Pharisee' prayed that his few sins might be deducted
from his many virtues. The 'thrifty—Pharisee' said:
'From my modest means I have something to perform
a good work.' Another said: 'Would that I knew of a
sin I had committed that I might perform an act of
virtue in atonement.' There was the 'Schechem—
Pharisee' who walked with his eyes shut lest the sight
of a woman might defile him, and who by doing so often
hit his nose against a post. These are Jewish caricatures
of Jews. It is caricatured with not only ludicrous exag-
geration but heightened and coloured by the most biting
sarcasm. The true Pharisees were Job and Abraham,
who were Rabbis for love of God. All these types may
be duplicated and multiplied in the most highly civilised
communities.

The self-righteous man measures himself by his neighbours. His opinion of them is small and his own spiritual stature is correspondingly low. In modern temples the words are not uttered—they are acted. Costumes and make-ups are large items. Russian sables costing hundreds of guineas would instantly lose their temple value if the lady's washer-woman could come to worship rigged out in the same way. Their value consists largely in the fact that there are few who can possess them. Two persons went into the (modern) temple to pray—the one a lady, the other a woman! or, the one a parasite, the other a worker! Such a basis for a parable would be just as objectionable to Christians as the parable of the Pharisee and the publican is to the Jews. It would be just as true, however. True to life It is just as easy to experiment in the spiritual laboratory as in the chemical.

It was with the publican, then, it is the publican now. The publican in the parable measures himself by the love of God, and, feeling acutely the long distance between him and the ideal, he cried out, 'God, be merciful to me, a sinner.' Money talks, clothes talk, titles talk, social standing talks—they talk loudly. That is one reason why the poor are silent. In the Kingdom these have no standing. It is the hearts desire that counts.

Labels are often libels. These two men were wrongly tagged. One was labelled good, and he was a fraud. The other was labelled bad, and Jesus commends him. And what He commends is the essence of the Kingdom.

The Pharisaic Spirit

Modern Pharisaism is as subtle as it was in Jerusalem. It is as widespread. It is likely to be found in the chapel as in the cathedral. The modern type is now, as then, more likely to be found in intellectuals The Pharisee is found in Congress, in the Chamber of Deputies, and in the House of Commons. He is the contemporary ancestor. Sometimes he is an ecclesiastic—the incumbent of a mausoleum of dead hopes. Sometimes the Pharisaic spirit is accentuated in the empty soul of a parasitic woman. The spirit of the Pharisee is manifested in pride of place, creed, sect, or building. It is the narrow 'holier than thou' attitude in society, politics or religion The Pharisee is a person who looks down on others, and up to himself. It is self-measurement by false standards. It is the outward show of pious phrases that covers the plague of a gangrened heart It ingratiates itself into the sacred precincts of the temple, but is excluded from the Kingdom whose standard of measurement is the Master Himself.

¶ 117

The Measure of Service

'But who is there of you, having a servant ploughing, or keeping sheep, that will say unto him, when he is come in from the field, Come straightway and sit down to meat; and will not rather say unto him, Make ready wherewith I may sup, and gird thyself, and serve me, till I have eaten and drunken; and afterwards thou shalt eat and drink. Doth he thank the servant, because he did the things that were commanded? Even so ye also, when ye shall have done all the things that are commanded you, say, We are unprofitable servants; we have done which it was our duty to do.'

Luke xvii. 7–10 (R V.).

From the temple we are led out into the open field. From the inflated egotist to the subservient slave. From the proud boast of performances to the slave shepherd watching his sheep. It is beyond our ken to imagine a modern ploughman or shepherd leaving the field or hillside, and transforming himself into a flunkey, to serve his master as a household menial. Our Western minds instantly pounce upon the transformation rather than

the parallel truth of the story. The story is a comment
on the Pharisee's numeration of works performed. He
thinks the angels might hold a mass meeting, and pass
a resolution of thanks to him for his beneficence. It is
an illustration from the ordinary life of the East.

Is it customary, He asks, for the master to wait on
the slaves, or for the slaves to wait on the master? Or
can you conceive of the master thanking his slave for
his services? Of course not. It is the other way about.
The relation is perfectly understood. But your relation
to the God of the Universe is not quite as well known.
They had left their vocation to follow Him, and for
that they wanted special emoluments here and hereafter. When you have done all that is in your power to
do—all that you are commanded—then you may truth-
fully say, 'We are unprofitable servants, for we have
only done which was our duty to do.' Humility is one
of the most beautiful graces of the Kingdom, and it is
the grace that whispers to the left hand, not on any
account to let the right hand know what it has been
doing. Pharisaism is its own sandwichman, placarding
its good deeds fore and aft. Service like prayer, is to be
done secretly and if genuinely done that way, receives
the open reward of the Father. Eye service and self-
seeking, have no reward. God won't be haggled with
on a this for that basis. 'Doth Job serve God for
naught?' Yes, certainly, that is the divine law.

¶ 118

Work and Wages

'The Kingdom of heaven is like unto a man
that is a householder, which went out early in
the morning to hire labourers into his vineyard.
And when he had agreed with the labourers for a
penny a day, he sent them into his vineyard. And
when he went out about the third hour, and saw
others standing in the market place idle; and to
them he said, Go ye also into the vineyard, and

whatsoever is right I will give you. And they went their way. Again he went out about the sixth and the ninth hour, and did likewise. And about the eleventh hour he went out, and found others standing; and he saith unto them, Why stand ye here all day idle? They say unto him, Because no man hath hired us. He saith unto them, Go ye also into the vineyard. And when even was come, the lord of the vineyard saith unto his steward, Call the labourers, and pay them their hire, beginning from the last unto the first. And when they came that were hired about the eleventh hour, they received every man a penny. And when the first came, they supposed they would receive more; and they likewise received every man a penny. And when they received it they murmured against the householder, saying, These last have spent but one hour, and thou hast made them equal unto us, which have borne the burden of the day and the scorching heat. But he answered and said to one of them, Friend, I do thee no wrong: didst thou not agree with me for a penny? Take up that which is thine, and go thy way; it is my will to give unto the last, even as unto thee. Is it not lawful for me to do what I will with mine own? or is thine eye evil, because I am good?'

Matthew xx. 1-15 (R.V.).

At first glance, the parable looks like an ethical discussion on labour and capital. We see one man working for eleven hours, and another working for one, and both getting the same pay—a penny. We look at the penny and surmise that it may mean a pound, but the disparity in the labour contribution is not so easily settled. The question is too acute with us to dismiss it as easily as the unknown value of a Roman penny.

The whole story is told to illustrate one point, an the point was succinctly stated after the telling of the parable: **'The last shall be first!'** The parable if adopted by business men or enacted into law as an Act of Parliament, would contribute nothing to labour or capital, but it might be a good point of departure for a revolution. Jesus is illuminating the workings of the law of the Kingdom. He sees a host of self-seeking and self-righteous people making claims to priority and special consideration. They want to lead the procession. He turns the procession around and marches it in tail end on! that is the point.

A crowd jostled and pushed each other roughly about in London the other day, trying hard with physical force to board a train. Each wanted to be first. At the back of the crowd stood a frail woman with a baby in her arms. The conductress with a woman's instinct, took the situation in at a glance. She stopped the rush and shouted, 'Gangway for that woman with the child!' The crowd was cowed, the rush ceased, and between two walls of shamed people the woman walked into the train and took a seat. That also is a point.

.   .   .   .   .   .

Those who at one time or another claimed leadership in the procession of the Kingdom were, the elder brother, the Pharisee of the temple, Simon the Pharisee, Salome and her sons. Others were equally respectable, equally good, and equally loud in claim or request. They placed themselves by self-estimate in the front rank. In the rear rank by their own estimate, also were ranged the prodigal, the publican, the woman taken in sin, the Capernaum woman of the streets, the tax-gatherers, sinners, nondescripts, the poor, and despised. There they stand self-placed. The law of the Kingdom gives the order, 'Right about turn!' The ranks are reversed and the rear rank marches in first! That is not a pleasant sight for front rankers, but that is the plain inference to be drawn from this and other parables of Jesus, and to the modern, religious mind it is almost unthinkable.

¶ 119

Courage and Deceit

'What think ye? A man had two sons; and he came to the first and said, Son, go work to-day in the vineyard. And he answered and said, I will not; but afterward he repented himself, and went. And he came to the second and said likewise. And he answered and said, I go, sir: and went not. Whether of the twain did the will of his father? They say, the first.'

Matthew xxi., 28–31a (R.V.).

The last part of verse 31 is the value of both parables. It is Jesus Himself reversing the ranks, and stating the reason for the reversal in specific terms.

Of the two sons, the one who had courage and frankness to tell his father the exact truth as he felt it at the time is the most commendable. The other lacked the courage and played the hypocrite. **'What think ye?'** He asks, **'which of these sons did the will of his father?'** They say, 'The first.'

He reminds them that John the Baptist came, came in their way, in the way of righteousness, came to warn them, but they believed him not. But the publicans and harlots believed him, here they stand, weighed in the balance with the offscouring of Galilee and Judæa. It is a question of values—spiritual values, and they are outweighed. The points of comparison have changed. It is the Christian religion of the twentieth century that is now in the balance being weighed, with the religion of the Kingdom. They were orthodox, they were scrupulously careful about the outward forms, rituals, and ceremonies, but because they were spiritually dead, the publicans and harlots would go into the Kingdom of God before them. That is the dictum of Jesus, not only to the formalists of ancient times, but to the formalists and Pharisees of modern times. They said they would go and didn't. The others at first refused point blank,

but later surrendered to love, and went.   In the Kingdom, the frankness of the bad is preferable to the deceit
of the good.

¶ 120

Solicitude for the Straying

**'How think ye?   If any man have a hundred
sheep, and one of them be gone astray, doth he
not leave the ninety-and-nine, and go unto the
mountains, and seek that which goeth astray?
and if so be that he find it, verily I say unto you,
he rejoiceth over it more than over the ninety-
and-nine which have not gone astray.   Even so
it is not the will of your Father which is in heaven, that one of these little ones should perish.'**
Matthew xviii. 12–14 (R.V.).

This is a literary as well as a spiritual gem.   It en-
shrines a cardinal truth of the Kingdom.   A shepherd
leaves the sheltered sheepfold where ninety-nine sheep
are safe, and goes out to the mountains in search of one
that is lost.   Either spoken or written, it is a fascinating
picture, and kindles the imagination of the dullest mind.
There were times when his naturally gentle tongue cut
like a rapier through the sham defences of His critics.
He could be violently angry without the slightest tinge of
personal resentment.   There were other times when His
tenderness must have moved them to the edge of tears.
This was one of them.   There are few passages in the
literature of Israel to equal the idyllic beauty of the
story of the lost sheep.   A passage in the song of Moses
probably is the nearest approach:—

> 'As an eagle stirreth up her nest,
> Fluttered over her young,
> Spreadeth abroad her wings,
> Taketh them,
> Beareth them on her wings.
> So the Lord did lead them.'

The Shepherd Heart

Tender solicitude is the theme in both cases. A sheep in the East is more than mutton. There springs up a relationship between the shepherd and his sheep that has been the theme of poets since Theocritus. The lambs are like little children and require care. A sheep astray is in danger. Enemies around with beak and claw ready to destroy and devour. No one knows this as well as the shepherd. No one feels the danger so keenly. So he takes risks. He crosses the valleys, goes through scrubs and climbs over the rocks to the slopes and edges of the mountains.

No animal is so utterly helpless, when astray, as a sheep. It has no scent, no sense of direction. It will follow no trail. Like a hen, it will run a short distance and suddenly stop! A flock and a shepherd are absolutely essential to its existence. We feel all this as we read the story. When he finds the sheep he rejoices, and we share his joy. He is more pleased over the recovery of one, than over the safety of the ninety-and-nine. The parallel truth is obvious throughout. The sinner who is astray is the wandering sheep. The shepherd is the Father. The ninety-and-nine are those who remain safely within the shelter of the fold. The joy of the shepherd who finds the wandering one, is the joy of the angels over the return to the fold of that which was lost. This is the defence of a love that never wanes, a love that has no limit, no strings attached, and is as unconditioned as the fall of the rain or the light of the sun that falls equally on the just and the unjust. It is a supplemental picture to the lost sheep—a revelation of the Master Himself as the shepherd of the souls of men.

¶ 121

Father and Son

'A certain man had two sons: and the younger of them said to his father, Father, give me the portion of thy substance that falleth to me. And he divided unto them his living. And not many days after the younger son gathered all together, and took his journey into a far country; and there he wasted his substance with riotous living. And when he had spent all, there arose a mighty famine in that country; and he began to be in want. And he went and joined himself to one of the citizens of that country; and he sent him into the fields to feed swine. And he would have fain been filled with the husks that the swine did eat; and no man gave unto him. But when he came to himself he said, 'How many hired servants of my father's have bread enough and to spare, and I perish here with hunger! I will arise and go to my father, and I will say unto him, Father, I have sinned against heaven and in thy sight: I am no more worthy to be called thy son: make me as one of thy hired servants.

And he arose and came to his father. But while he was yet afar off, his father saw him, and was moved with compassion and ran and fell on his neck, and kissed him. And the son said unto him, Father, I have sinned against heaven and in thy sight: I am no more worthy to be called thy son. But the father said to his servants, Bring forth quickly the best robe, and put it on him; and put a ring on his hand, and shoes on his feet, and bring the fatted calf, and kill it, and let us eat, and make merry: for this my son was dead, and is alive again; and he was lost and is found. And they began to be merry. Now his elder son was in the field: and he came and drew nigh to the house, he heard music and dancing. And he called one of the servants and inquired what these things might be. And he said unto him, Thy brother is come; and thy father hath killed the fatted calf, because he hath received him safe and sound. But he was angry, and would not go in; and his father came out and entreated him. But he answered and said to his father, Lo, these many years do I serve thee, and I never transgfessed a commandment of thine: and yet thou never gavest me a kid, that I might make merry with my friends; but when this thy son came, which hath devoured thy living with harlots, thou killest for him the fatted calf. And he said unto him, Son, thou art ever with me, and all that is mine is thine, but it was meet to make merry and be glad; for this thy brother was dead and is alive again; and was lost and is found.

Luke xv. 11–32 (R.V.).

The parable of the lost sheep, of the lost coin, of the lost man, are one parable in three sections. One of one hundred, one of ten, one of two. The first was lost by accident, the second by ignorance, the third went astray deliberately. All of them illustrate the love of the Father for the wanderer.

The woman who lost one of the ten coins, lit a candle and searched diligently until she found it. Then she called her neighbours and they rejoiced with her. It is an Eastern story and to us unusual. The parallel truth is more obvious than the story itself.

.   .   .   .   .   .

The parable of the prodigal is an epitome of the Kingdom. It is all there. The erring heart, the sickness with sin, the balancing of spiritual accounts, the decision for right, the return and the welcome of the Father, whose love never flagged or wavered. A marked feature of these word pictures of the Kingdom is the rejoicing over the wanderer's return. The reference to the older brother is a reproof of the religious world—arrogant, austere, hard, and out of touch, and sympathy with those for whom the Father's heart eternally hungers.

The Most Beautiful Story

This is the most beautiful story, the most perfect and the most instructive of all the pictures with which He illuminated the Kingdom. The prodigal knows nothing of dogmas, ordinances, or institutions. He is caught by no catch-words, enamoured of no propaganda. This is the last word—the ultimate belief in the relation of man to God, and God to man. In the simplest possible language the basic elements of religion are revealed. The theologians have contended that Jesus meant His message of the Kingdom to be taken provisionally. They assume that the living message was to undergo a re-interpretation after His death. It did, and some fundamental aspects of His message—some of His profoundest sayings—were put aside as of little account. This comes very near making Him a mere factor in the Kingdom—a forerunner of theologians. The outside world is brushing aside sophistry, and going back to Him as the Way, the Truth, and the Life—the founder, the power, and the personal realisation of the Kingdom.

The obvious parallel truth is this: we sow the wind and reap the whirlwind. A moment of reflection comes. We weigh the results—spurious pleasures in one scale, real pleasures in the other. The desires of the flesh are not what they seemed. We become sated. The desires of the spirit are truth, goodness, and beauty. When sated with the lower, we crave the higher. The will to return is all that is needed. We leave the domain of flesh and start out in quest of the spirit.

That quest brings us back to the Father, and there He stands as we left Him, loving us as if we had never gone astray. The eternal and unchangeable love of the Father for every erring child is the sum total of the parable. All the rest is detail. What a wonderful picture! Jesus said it, and His word is final!

¶ 122

The Seed and the Soil

'Hearken: Behold, the sower went forth to sow, and it came to pass, as he sowed some seed fell by the wayside, and the birds came and devoured it. And others fell on the rocky ground, where it had not much earth; and straightway it sprung up, because it had no deepness of earth: and when the sun was risen, it was scorched; and because it had no root, it withered away. And others fell among the thorns, and the thorns grew up and choked it, and it yielded no fruit. And others fell into the good ground, and yielded fruit, growing up and increasing; and brought forth thirtyfold, and sixtyfold, and a hundredfold. And he said, Who hath ears to hear, let him hear.'

Mark iv. 3–9 (R.V.).

Mark calls the above parable 'His doctrine.' Not the 'ornamental fringe' or something subject to revision later, but 'His doctrine.' A great crowd pressed upon Him by the seaside, and in order to give His voice the greatest possible range, He got into a boat, and at this point of advantage He taught them. His reference to seed is well understood. The story is universal. So is the parallel truth—the truth that the spiritual seed of the Kingdom finds different measures of receptivity in the hearts of men. The Master explains in detail the meaning, though none of His parables are more obvious. The truth contained in it is too important to be associated with the slightest doubt. So He explains: **'The seed is the word of God. The seed that fell by the wayside are those that bear, then cometh Satan and taketh away the seed lest they should believe and be saved. The seed that fell on the rock are those who receive the word with joy but having no root, believe only for a while, then when temptation comes they fall away. The seed that fell among thorns are they which, when they have heard, go forth, but the cares, riches, and pleasures of this life choke them, and they cannot bring forth any fruit to perfection. But the seed that falls on good ground are those who in an honest and good heart, having heard the word keep it and bring forth fruit in patience.'** What then is 'the word of God?' It is not a book, nor an institution. It is the message that Jesus is delivering —that God is Love, that to Him every individual soul has a value. The realisation that God is a loving Father produces spiritual fruit—like produces like, love begets love—and the fruit is loving the Father, and loving others as He loves us, or as we love ourselves.

A Postscript

Is the lamp there
To be under a bushel
Or under a bed?
And not on a stand?
For nothing is hid
Save to make it more plain;
And nothing concealed
Save to bring it to light.
Who hath ears to hear
Let him hear!

And take heed how ye hear!
With what measure ye mete
To you is it measured.
Yea, more shall be added;
For to him that hath
To him shall be given;
To him that hath not
From him shall be taken,
Even that which he hath!

¶ 123

The Mystery of Growth

'So is the Kingdom of God, as if a man should
cast seed upon the earth, and should sleep and
rise night and day and the seed should spring up
and grow, he knoweth not how. The earth bear-
eth fruit of herself, first the blade, then the ear,
then the full corn in the ear. But when the fruit
is ripe, straightway he putteth forth the sickle,
because the harvest is come.'

Mark iv. 26–29 (R.V.).

'The wind bloweth where it listeth, thou hearest
the sound thereof but canst not tell whence it
cometh or whither it goeth. So is everyone that
is born of the spirit.' The seed in the ground seems
to rot, but there is a live germ. Earth and moisture
open the envelope and the life comes forth. Then
sunshine nourishes the blade, then comes the ear,
then the full corn in the ear. It is all a mystery. The
growth of the spiritual life is as mysterious as the life
of nature. Men do not quarrel over the mystery of
growth in nature, and yet despite the fact that Jesus
warned His followers that it was a mystery, and that we
could no more tell accurately the operation of love in
the heart, than we could tell the whence and whether
of the wind. His followers have murdered each other

because growth could not be made uniform! The lesson of the parable is the secret, mysterious, and unsearchable character of the Kingdom's growth in the human heart.

¶ 124

The Kingdom's Power of Expansion

'Unto what is the Kingdom of God like? and whereunto shall I liken it? It is like unto a grain of mustard seed, which a man took, and cast into his own garden; and it grew, and became a tree; and the birds of the heaven lodged in the branches thereof.'

Luke xiii. 18–19 (R.V.).

One little candle lights many other candles. One heart on fire sets many other hearts on fire, one full of joy gives joy to others. Jesus sowed the seed of the Kingdom in the hearts of a few men in Galilee, and the seed grew, and increased an hundredfold, and it was sown again in other hearts in other lands, and the harvest is not yet. Every heart is a seed-bed of the Kingdom— a centre of life, a source of influence. All that is necessary is the seed, and the seed is the word of God. The expansion of the Kingdom is the expansion and diffusion of love. That is the lesson of the grain of mustard seed.

¶ 125

The Power of Leaven

'Whereunto shall I liken the Kingdom of God? It is like unto leaven, which a woman took and hid in three measures of meal until it was all leavened.'

Luke xiii. 20–21 (R.V.).

The parable of the leaven is a development of the parable of the mustard seed. The leaven gives life to the inert mass. It permeates every atom. Quiet, potent, and all-pervasive is the power of the Kingdom. Working from within, out, it raises the tone, sweetens the atmosphere, and transforms into its likeness whatever it comes in contact with.

¶ 126

The Problem of Good and Evil

'The Kingdom of heaven is likened unto a man that sowed good seed in his field; but while men slept, his enemy came, and sowed tares also among the wheat, and went away. But when the blades sprang up and brought forth fruit, then appeared the tares also. And the servants of the householder came and said to him, Sir, didst thou not sow good seed in thy field? whence then hath it tares? And he said unto them, An emeny hath done this. And the servants said unto him, Wilt thou then that we go and gather them up? But he saith, Nay; lest haply while ye gather up the tares, ye root up the wheat with them. Let both grow, together until the harvest, and in the time of the harvest I will say to the reapers, Gather up first the tares and bind them in bundles to burn them, but gather the wheat into my barn.'

Matthew xiii. 24–30 (R.V.)

The parable of the tares and the drag net, have the same lesson. They are different views on the same subject. A net cast into the sea is drawn in upon the beach, and the fishermen proceed to divide the good from the bad. The good they keep and the bad they cast away. In some countries manure is made of bad fish. It is a good fertiliser. In the case of the tares, an enemy sowed them. They grew up with the wheat and when the servants saw them they informed the master and asked whether they should take them out? They were instructed to let them grow, and at the end of the harvest they would be gathered together and burnt in a rubbish heap.

The light on the Kingdom here is that life is for fruit-bearing and not for summary Judgment. It is for building not for destruction. It is more than likely that the parables of the tares was the last of the series, and naturally deals with last things. There would be counterfeit citizens in the Kingdom, but to root them out would divert attention and hinder the building process. There would come a day of reckoning, when the chaff would be sifted from the wheat. A hypocrite is the architect of his own ruin—let him build, is the injunction—he builds on the sand. Let him alone. For the present the practical test is fruit. Later, His followers abandoned His breadth of Judgment and burnt at the stake not hypocrites and mammon worshippers, but saints of the Kingdom, who were distinguished for piety and purity of life. The ecclesiastical racks and thumb-screws have gone into the discard, for the reason that a civilisation more akin to the Kingdom than their users, put a stop to their use. History records, and not infrequently, the fact that the world with a sword in its hand has forced the church to adopt the humanities of the Kingdom.

RESPONSIBILITY AND JUDGMENT

¶ 127

The Unusual Guests

Preface

And He said to him
Also that had bidden Him,
'When thou makest a dinner

Or a supper, call not
Thy friends, nor thy brethren,
Nor thy rich kinsmen,
Nor rich neighbours;
Lest haply they bid thee
Again, and a recompense
Be made thee.
But when thou makest
A feast, bid the poor,
The maimed, the lame,
The blind: and thou
 shalt be blessed:
Because they have not
The wherewith to recompense
 thee, for thou shalt
Be recompensed in
The resurrection of
The just.'

Jesus as a guest in the home of a chief Pharisee is discoursing on the kind of hospitality that becometh the Kingdom. When He had finished what is here arranged as a preface to the parable, one of those who sat at meat with Him said: 'Blessed is he that shall eat bread in the Kingdom of God.' Then He told this story:—

'A certain man made a great supper; and he bade many: and he sent forth his servants at supper time to say to them that were bidden, Come, for all things are now ready. And they all with one consent began to make excuses. The first said unto then, I have bought a field, and I must needs go and see it: I pray thee have me excused. And another said, I have bought five yoke of oxen, and I go to prove them: I pray thee have me excused. And another said, I have married a wife, and therefore I cannot come. And the servant came and told his lord these things. Then the master of the house, being angry, said to his servant, Go out quickly into the streets and lanes of the city, and bring in hither the poor, and the maimed, and the blind, and lame. And the servant said, Lord what thou didst command is done, and yet there is room. And the lord said unto the servant, Go into the highways and hedges and constrain them to come in, that my house may be filled. For I say unto you, that none of those men which were bidden shall taste of my supper.'

Luke xiv. 16-24 (R.V.).

There is a democratic atmosphere here that would ill suit the unctuous Pharisees of any age. The instruction in the preface is direct and unmistakable. Nothing veiled, nothing obscure. It is about the only teaching of Jesus over which Christians have not fought. All sects are thoroughly agreed on it, and all have ignored it. Between the feasts of the pagan and the idle rich, and the feasts of the Christians, there is absolutely no line of demarcation—no distinction. It is unthinkable in modern life that at a social function of any sort or description the injunction of Jesus should receive any serious consideration. This is where the line of clearage between the Kingdom and the Church is most marked. If a prophet of God with the fire of John the Baptist, and the spiritual fervour of Paul should come forth and ask the leading members of the modern church why they never even pretended to follow Jesus in this matter, he would be looked upon as a fool or a madman! When a feast is made we call our 'Kinsmen,' our 'friends,' our 'brethren,' and our 'rich neighbours' (if we think they will accept and return the compliment). These are the classes of guests that recompense us by asking us back. 'Ask the poor, the maimed, the lame, and the blind,' Jesus says, 'they will not be able to ask you to their homes in return, but I will recompense you at the resurrection of the just.'

Simply and pungently Jesus teaches in the parable that into the new social order of the Kingdom a rich and respectable world will not enter. They may enter the church, for no such demands are made on them there. Some sects in order to lower the standards and admit them, have proclaimed themselves the Kingdom and labelled all others as schismatics and heretics.

. . . . . .

We give alms, and provide soup kitchens. We give our old clothes. But that falls short of the Kingdom's plain command of a democratic spiritual kindness, by which we are asked by the Master to invite the really poor and needy to our feasts. We cannot get around it, save by a Pharisaic casuistry that He encountered in the days of His sojourn on earth.

There is another aspect of this higher teaching which, if considered, might give added incentive to obey the new law. The spiritually minded, acting from the purest motives in inviting the needy, invite Jesus Himself, for He said, **'Inasmuch as ye do it unto one of the least of these my little ones, ye do it unto me.'**

¶ 128

Religion in Rags

'Now there was a certain rich man, and he was clothed in purple and fine linen, faring sumptuously every day: and a certain beggar named Lazarus was laid at his gate, full of sores, and desiring to be fed with the crumbs that fell from the rich man's table; yea, even the dogs came and licked his sores. And it came to pass, that the beggar died, and that he was carried away by the angels into Abraham's bosom; and the rich man also died and was buried. And in Hades he lifted up his eyes, being in torment, and seeth Abraham afar off, and Lazarus in his bosom. And he cried, and said, Father Abraham, have mercy on me, and send Lazarus that he may dip the tip of his finger in water, and cool my tongue; for I am in anguish in this flame. But Abraham said, Son, remember that thou in thy life time receivest thy good things, and Lazarus in like manner evil things; but now here he is comforted, and thou art in anguish. And beside all this, between us and you there is a great gulf fixed, that they which would pass from hence to you may not be able, and none may cross over from hence to us. And he said, I pray thee therefore, father, that thou wouldst send him to my father's house; for I have five brethren; that he may testify unto them, lest they also come unto this place of torment. But Abraham saith, They have Moses and the prophets; let them hear them. And he said, Nay, Father Abraham; but if one go to them from the dead they will repent. And he said unto him, If they hear not Moses and the prophets, either, will they be persuaded, if one rises from the dead.'

Luke xvi. 19-31 (R.V.).

Lazarus is a concrete illustration of 'Blessed are ye poor.' The rich man lived in luxury. Lazarus lay at his door, eating crumbs if he could get them, and the dogs licked his sores. It's a gruesome picture The. two kingdoms are close together. The Kingdom of the stomach and the Kingdom of the heart, of purple and fine linen and rags. The parable is neither a condemnation of riches, as such, not a sanction of poverty. It's a statement of conditions with an uncovering of the foundations on which they rest. Social conditions may rob a man of foods and clothes, but they cannot deprive him of the Kingdom of God. The parable is a highly coloured picture of Jewish religious thought. It is not a guide to a future life. 'Abraham's Bosom' is a picturesque expression describing the abode of the blest. The disparity on earth is equalised in heaven, but the decisions governing the future are made here. The lesson is plain. The basic values are appraised. In justice, greed and wanton luxury have an end. The mills of God grind slowly—but they grind. The rich man's first thought for others comes to him in hell. Even then he thinks of his own class—not the class whose comfort comes largely from the dogs on the street. He thinks of himself and his kinsmen. He wants them warned, and for himself he asks that Lazarus provide a drop of cold water to cool his tongue. He is told that if his kinsmen hear not Moses and the prophets neither will they believe though one rise from the dead.

No fine spun web of doctrine can be woven out of the details of this story. A broad general principle is laid down—a principle as applicable now as then. Dives still lives. So does Lazarus. Hovels and palaces, rags, and fine linen, riches and poverty are now, as then, in close juxtaposition. Dives was respectable and rich, and undoubtedly religious, but he went to hell, nevertheless. Lazarus was sore and poor and outcast but he belonged to the Kingdom. That is the lesson. Over the gulf which divides men into two camps—the haves and have-nots, the hungry and the overglutted, a bridge is being built—the bridge is Justice. Citizens of the Kingdom, both rich and poor are the builders. Meantime Jesus stands with the poor. The Kingdom is theirs.

¶ 129

Lamps Without Oil

'Then shall the Kingdom of heaven be likened unto ten virgins, which took their lamps, and went forth to meet the bridegroom. And five of them were foolish, and five were wise. For the foolish, when they took their lamps, took no oil with them: but the wise took oil in their

vessels with their lamps. Now while the bridegroom tarried, they all slumbered and slept.
But at midnight there is a cry, Behold the bridegroom! Come ye forth to meet him. Then all
those virgins arose and trimmed their lamps.
And the foolish said unto the wise, Give us of
your oil; for our lamps are going out. But the
wise answered, saying, Peradventure there will
be not enough for us and you: go ye rather to
them that sell, and buy for yourselves. And
while they went away to buy, the bridegroom
came; and they that were ready went in with
him to the marriage feast: and the door was
shut. Afterwards came also the other virgins,
saying, Lord, lord, open unto us. But he answered and said, Verily I say unto you, I know
you not, Watch, therefore, for ye know not the
day nor the hour.'

Matthew xxv. 1-13 (R.V.).

In the Kingdom the Bridegroom comes every day:
The parable warns us to be ready. When 'they all
forsook him, and fled.' Their lamps had gone out,
Peter had no oil when he denied him. Thoughtlessness,
heedlessness, and neglect of the things that matter, may
not damn us but they empty our lives of the joy of
service. When love is on guard the sentry is not asleep.
When the angel of opportunity comes love stands at
the door, ready to open it. Eternal vigilance is the
price of liberty of soul as well as in the march of the
democratic ideal down the centuries. In the Kingdom,
the word is 'Watch.' Of all epitaphs—'too late' is the
saddest.

¶ 130

The Buried Opportunity

'A man going into another country, called his
own servants, and delivered unto them his goods.
And unto one he gave five talents, to another two,

to another one; each according to his several
abilities; and he went on his journey. Straightway he that received the five talents went and
traded with them, and made other five talents.
In like manner he that received the two gained
other two. But he that received the one went
away and digged in the earth, and hid his lord's
money. Now after a long time the lord of those
servants cometh, and maketh a reckoning with
them. And he that received the five talents came
and brought other five talents, saying, Lord, thou
deliverest unto me five talents: lo, I have gained
other five talents. His lord said unto him, Well
done thou good and faithful servant: thou hast
been faithful over a few things, I will set thee
over many things: enter thou into the joy of thy
lord. And he also that received the two talents
came and said, Lord, thou deliverest unto me
two talents: lo, I have gained other two talents.
His lord said unto him, Well done, good and
faithful servant, thou hast been faithful over a
few things, I will set thee over many things:
enter thou into the joy of thy lord. And he also
that received the one talent came and said, Lord,
I knew thee that thou art a hard man, reaping
where thou didst not sow, and gathering where
thou didst not scatter: and I was afraid, and
went away and hid thy talent in the earth: lo,
thou hast thine own. But his lord answered and
said unto him, Thou wicked and slothful servant, thou knewest I reap where I sowed not,
and gather where I did not scatter; thou oughtest
therefore to have put my money to the bankers,
and at my coming I should have received back
mine own with interest. Take ye away therefore
the talent from him, and give it unto him that
hath ten talents. For unto every one that hath
shall be given, and he shall have abundance; but
from him that hath not, even that which he

hath shall be taken away. And cast ye out the unprofitable servant into outer darkness: there shall be weeping and gnashing of teeth.'

Matthew xxv. 14-30 (R.V.).

The parable of the talents is not 'a handy guide to safe investments.' Not infrequently it has been so understood. Because Jesus takes a moneylender as the basis of his story He has been understood as endorsing the business. The story is one of responsibility and judgment. It is an illustration—not a commendation. The talents of the Kingdom are not coins but gifts and graces A gift or grace unused is buried. When used they multiply.

When the man with one talent told his master that he reaped where he had not sown and gathered where he had not scattered, he told him the truth. The capitalist acknowledges the truth, but expostulates and says: 'Yes, of course, but you knew that when I entrusted you with the talent! you knew that, when I went away, why then did you assume the responsibility? Why didn't you give it to my banker, so that when I returned I would have had my principal and my usury?' The parable truth is quite obvious. In the Kingdom we are entrusted with talents of another kind. With even the smallest we assume responsibility. If we use what is given, we are given more and greater. For every gift and grace we bury or misuse, we are called to judgment. Every citizen of the Kingdom is judge of his own stewardship, but there will come a final summing up of what we have done or left undone.

The money lender and the man with one talent were both actuated by selfish motives. The gifts of the Kingdom are profitable, but they have no cash value. The king is not a userer. He scatters abroad and gathers not for Himself. He sows for His friends to reap. In one case it was a cold business proposition— in the other it was a community of interest in things spiritual. It was an investment of influence, of love and kindness.

CHAPTER XII

The Emotions of the Master

¶ *131*

Anger

The anger of Jesus was a passionate resentment. The profanation of the Temple made Him angry and He whipped the profaners out of its precincts. He was angry at the Hypocrisy of the Pharisees and He used a vocabulary that must have stung them to the quick. **"Ye compass sea and land to make one proselyte, and when ye have made him, he is two-fold more the child of Hell than yourselves!"** That is anger and perhaps tinged with bitterness, but the element of revenge is absent. His heart burned like a flame of fire for the true, the good and the beautiful, and the consciousness that the custodians of morals were "White Sepulchres" made Him angry. The leaders of the people were extortioners, traitors to the highest and oppressors of the weak. His anger therefore was but a phase of His burning love.

His capacity for anger was continually tested, but seldom did He deviate from His calm dignity. When He burst forth in violent indignation He struck terror to the hearts of hypocrites and oppressors and at the same time enthused and gave courage to the common people who thronged Him everywhere.

"Ye blind guides which strain at a gnat, and swallow a camel."
"Ye fools and blind!
"Woe unto you, Scribes and Pharisees, Hypo-

crites, for ye make clean the outside of the cup and platter, but within they are full of extortion and excess.

"Ye serpents, ye generation of vipers, how can ye escape the damnation of hell?

"Scribes, Pharisees, Hypocrites, Ye shut up the Kingdom of Heaven against men, for ye neither go in yourselves neither suffer ye them that are entering to go in.

"Depart from me ye cursed!"

As concentrated, penetrative, burning invective, the above has seldom been equalled. It is vituperation but not abuse. It is castigation and verbal damnation but without either pique or petulance.

Anger is a two edged sword and a dangerous weapon in the hands of ordinary men. It is an emotion which, when indulged, poisons and corrupts the motive that prompts it. Often it blinds the reason and becomes in essence the thing it storms against. Anger can only be justified when it springs from a heart aflame with holiness. With Jesus it was indignant resentment to the oppression of the poor, and the shams of a perverted religious system. With us it is more often just common ordinary bad temper, or a gnarled disposition, and we exercise the emotion only when our personal comfort is in danger of disturbance.

When He was reviled, He reviled not again. He took little notice of personal attacks upon Himself. They accused Him of gluttony, Sabbath breaking, wine-bibbing and many other things. To these accusations He replied with dignity, courtesy and calmness. With Him love and anger were opposite poles of the same thing. His anger was love outraged and hot with indignation.

In expressing the emotion of anger He was in direct personal contact with His antagonists. He cleansed the Temple single handed; but the force exerted was spiritual. It was the moral majesty of His anger that drove the money changers out. It was a loving heart that tipped

His tongue with fire. The Temple was His father's house of prayer. They had made it a den of thieves.

Yet anger was a mere incident to His ministry. Love was the dominant note—and its appeal never failed with the multitude. His anger was a necessity, not only to rebuke wrong, but to demonstrate to His followers and to the world that He was Human!

He was no alarmist. No demagogue—no inciter to violence, no mob leader, but the God-man in white anger shattering the shams with a voice that smote the conscience of men with terrific force. He lived in the midst of a crowd. He walked the streets. Anyone could interview Him at any time. His life was like a broad stream of quiet waters giving life and healing to the multitude, but when the river reached the rocks of sham, unbelief, oppression and lies, it formed a foaming cataract and that cataract was His anger.

¶ 132

Compassion

'If I had to be tried for a crime, and I could select a jury to try me,' said a literary man to me once, 'I would rather select a jury of publicans or a jury of harlots than a jury of either clergymen or deacons.'

'Why?' I asked.

'Because, from my experience, I am sure I would find more of the compassion of Jesus in these groups than I would find in Churchmen,' was the reply.

How common such an extraordinary idea may be is hard to tell, but it is neither negligible nor unique. It jars our complacency as the words of Jesus must have jarred the good elders of Jerusalem when Jesus told them that the harlots would enter the Kingdom ahead of them.

Compassion is the sharing of another's burden. It is looking at the situation from the sufferer's point of view. More than that, it is seeing as God sees. Jesus had compassion on the multitude. When they were hungry He fed them—fed them all, good, bad, and indifferent. He had compassion on the sick and healed them. To the harlot He said, **'Neither do I condemn thee, go and sin no more.'** He was not blind to sin. He knew its destructive power, but He also knew the long pathways along which these human failings had travelled. He saw men and women as dupes and victims struggling under a foreign yoke, a false religious system or a perverted nature within. In giving compassion, He gave Himself. He saw clear through Judas, but He gave Judas his chance. He reminded the woman at the well about her past only because she was quibbling about things that did not matter. It was not His custom to remind men and women of their past.

Sceptics, crooked business men, rationalists, traitors, ritualists, prostitutes, thieves, lawyers, the halt, the maimed, the blind, the bereaved, and the broken-hearted, were all the recipients of His compassion. He was called 'the friend of sinners.' He gave rest to the weary, food to the hungry, and hope to those in despair. Around the weaknesses in men He wrapped His strength. In the sheepfold of humanity He was partial to the sheep that were black. The Son of God had time to go about doing good. We have adapted labour-saving machinery in the things of the spirit. Much of our compassion is institutionalised. We arrange it in water-tight compartments, and dole it out in packets to those who are 'worthy.' The extra-ordinary compassion of the Master is of course explained away by the theologians. We are told that He mixed His communion with condemnation, but we are not told when or where. To read some of the commentators, one would imagine that Jesus cudgelled the sinner with one hand, while He embraced him with the other. The perplexed philosophers cannot quite make it out. His compassion does not quite fit into their cut-and-dried scheme of salvation. If Jesus did to-day what He did then, our best people would say He was encouraging crime! They did not understand Him then. They

would not understand Him now. The poor and the
needy and the outcast understood and loved Him, and
they would appreciate Him as much to-day as they did
then.

> 'Who gives himself with his alms gives three.
> Himself, his hungry brother, and me.'

¶ 133

Wonder

The word 'marvel' has long since lost the force it
possessed when the Scholars in the Jerusalem Chamber
used it to express the wonder of Jesus. Out of com-
parative obscurity came the word 'Wonder' to take
its place. The emotion of wonder is made up of many
sensations. According to our word-makers, wonder
expresses less than astonishment and much less than
amazement. It differs from admiration in not being
necessarily accompanied with love, esteem, or approbation. Common usage, however, has allied wonder
with astonishment, surprise, awe, horror, and also
with intense admiration.

Jesus wondered at the unbelief of the multitude.
He wondered at the Faith of a Roman soldier. In
one case the emotion was accompanied with a strong
feeling of admiration—in the other, by sadness. In
the solitudes His wonder was mingled with awe.

In a life of such spiritual adventure, wonder plays
a large part. The elements of surprise, astonishment,
and unexpectedness enter in. He wondered at the
aptness of some disciples and at the dullness and obtuse-
ness of others.

As I write there comes to my mind a scene in France.

On the way from Doulers to Cambrai in a motor-car
one day, my driver stopped at an army garage in a
small village. Two men were engaged in an argument.
It appeared that one of them had been sent from Corps
H.Q. to do repair work. There were seven cars in

'dry dock,' all of them in need of repair and useless. The man in charge could not repair them. He was there as caretaker—to see that nobody ran away with them. Here was a mechanic sent to get them into use again, but the caretaker refused to let him touch them. He questioned the mechanic's authority, then he questioned the source of it. They were both soldiers, they both knew that cars were in great demand, but red tape and stupidity stood in the way. We gave the mechanic a lift on his way back. 'Did you ever see anything so stupid?' he asked

The wonder of Jesus was of just such a character. He came to give facility, power, and usefulness to the machinery of life, and men haggled and quibbled over it. Compared to the casuistry of the Jewish ritual, the message of Jesus was the essence of simplicity. The multitude knew that it worked. They saw examples of the power in the lives of fishermen, tax-gatherers, and nondescripts. He was not asking them to give up the Temple or betray allegiance. Dry ritual had failed, stereotyped ceremonies added no zest to the dull routine of daily life. Jesus offered beauty for ashes, the oil of joy for the spirit of heaviness, and they looked at Him as dull oxen look at a dog with suspicion and fear.

So He wondered at their unbelief, and His wonder was mingled with sadness and surprise. It was the wonder of a man whose food is refused by the starving.

The wonder superinduced by the discovery of Faith where it was least expected, was accompanied by gladness and surprise. The Jews had a spiritual background. The Roman religion was barren and without hope. Where He expected warmth and receptivity, He found coldness and disdain. Here was a member of a foreign race, a soldier of an army whose very presence was a symbol of subjection and slavery, and in this man, Jesus found greater faith than He had found even amongst His immediate followers, and He marvelled with gladness at the discovery. To less discerning minds, the Master's estimate of the Centurion must in itself have been a cause for wonder. He alone could see the working

of the Roman mind which gave such a quick response
to the facts as they presented themselves to His sense
perceptions, but his interpretation of the influence
of Jesus was an act of faith that transcended the senses.
'O little faithed ones,' He said when His followers
were panic-stricken with fear. A moment before,
they were calm, and like ships in a harbour of refuge.
Now in a moment of physical danger they resembled
rudderless small craft at the mercy of a storm. He
marvelled at their instability. As they went up or
down in the scale of spiritual values, He went with
them in sadness or gladness, completely human as
they were, in physical pain or pleasure.

The emotionless man is an expressionless man. The
emotions of Jesus stand out as full expressions of the
life behind them. The New Testament writers were
engrossed with what they considered the larger aspects
of His life and teachings. His emotions were mentioned
incidentally. To men of these later days they are all
important. They are clues to His humanity and they
touch and influence the emotional life of mankind.

¶ 134

Joy

'Happiness,' Dr. Johnson said, 'is the multiplicity
of agreeable consciousness.' An element of that consciousness is the pleasure of having an aim in life. The
will of God was the supreme aim of the life of Jesus.
Whether He was sad or glad, exalted in spirit, or cast
down, whatever the varying circumstances of life
brought to Him, that consciousness remained as the
foundation of life and the background of all His varied
activities.

Joy is an emotion of pleasure. In common life we
associate the word with exultation, or with the sudden
gratification of desire. When we think of the joy of
Jesus, we are somehow unable to think of it as anything

but happiness intensified to such a degree, that it suffuses with the radiance of peace and love the entire personality.

If the juxtaposition of dissimilar propositions is the basis of laughter, I am sure Jesus must have laughed and laughed often. The New Testament writers seem to have considered laughter as unbecoming to the serious Messianic life, and that thought, that impression, has been so thoroughly hammered into our minds that we have excluded it from our conception of the Master, and to that extent have taken away from Him that which is normal in every human life.

In the Old Testament God laughs. So do Abraham and Sarah. In the New Testament Jesus promises laughter for tears. In both we get abundant records of how the race boiled over in wickedness, but scant reference to joyousness bubbling over into laughter.

The joy of Jesus is described explicitly and with a definiteness that leaves no room for doubt.

That He was a man of sorrow, and acquainted with grief, is in no wise incompatible with the fact that He was a man of joy.

There is probably no better exemplification in modern times of how the elements of joy and sadness may mix in a human personality, than in the life of Abraham Lincoln. A great artist who spent six months in the White House, said that Lincoln's face was the saddest face he had ever seen. And yet in the saddest moments of his country's peril, when its destiny hung in the balance, he would tell a funny story to divert the sorrow of those around him.

To make a catalogue of virtues—Trust, Hope, Obedience, etc., and say that the joy of Jesus was based on them, looks trivial, theological, and weak. The life of Jesus was no psychological chest of drawers ticketed with these things.

As a Galilean carpenter, builder, and cabinet-maker, He was a workman who needed not to be ashamed of His work. That in itself makes a solid foundation for joy. But when He left the carpenter's bench, He went out into the larger mission of life in the consciousness that His life was of the same texture as the life of God, and His joy deepened and widened as it flowed into the lives of men.

After that, His sadness was the flitting of a dark shadow over the face of the sunlit sea. An abiding joy became the essence of temperament—an emotion touched with the divine and an expression of an immortal love.

This joy He gave His followers. This joy becomes the possession of all men whose main purpose is linked with Him Joy in Him became contagious. It was as if He had opened a private door and walked into men's hearts. When full of His Joy, they spoke with His tongue, thought with His mind, and loved with His heart.

¶ 135

Genialness

There is a species of rose cultivated and brought to perfection by cutting away all buds on the stem but one. To this single bud goes the nourishment intended for the many. Something of that nature happens in the lives of some great saints. Their burning zeal for a single ideal burns up everything else in their natures.

Men of one idea are not infrequently censorious, over-critical, and crabbed in social relations. The world owes much to the men who fought for great ideals, but few of us would like to live with them. I glory in their achievements, but Jesus and Abraham Lincoln are the ones I would have liked to live with. The Master was genial. Geniality is a joyous social temperament It is cheerfulness with a generous admixture of sympathy, cordiality, and helpfulness.

The New Testament writers in describing the pathway of the soul, make it very largely a way of weeping. They give us an atmosphere of gloom, penetrated only here and there with sunshine. We know that Paul had a thorn in the flesh but we have no evidence that he ever laughed, nor have we any hint that he was genial.

Toplady, the author of 'Rock of Ages,' cudgelled the saintly Fletcher and described John Wesley, a still more saintly saint, as: 'An old fox tarred and feathered.' Paul, who wrote the greatest definition of Love ever written, had a passage at arms with Peter. Details are lacking as to the precise language used, but it seems to have been quite hot.

Jesus attended a wedding. His presence there is recorded, not so much to record His genial intercourse at a joyful feast as to prove Him a wonderworker. The modern mind is infinitely more interested in the fact that His genial personality fused genially and harmoniously with all sorts and conditions of men and women and little children.

When Matthew Levi celebrated his conversion by gathering together a nondescript group at a supper, Jesus was there to make them feel comfortable and at home. He never waited until they thought as He thought or did as He did. He loved the multitude and He loved them individually. He loved the rich young ruler even as He looked upon him.

Jesus had a genius for geniality. It was the charm of His genial companionship that bound to Him His followers. He is reported to have said that His followers would do greater things than He had done Himself. In all the Christian centuries we have records of very few who were noted for geniality. St Francis is probably more like him in this respect than any other.

That He should be imbued with the sublime idea of tenderly and lovingly changing the heart of the human race toward God and yet have time and inclination to be genial to folks around His shop, on the roadsides and on the streets is an eternal paradox.

Men who have no time for geniality have little time to be followers of Jesus. The separation of things into compartments of sacred and profane was unknown to

Him.   All things were sacred when put to a sacred use. The best and finest that was in Him spoke to a kindred value in the hearts of men around Him.   He saw good in men who could not see it in themselves.

At this candle of geniality, men lit their little lights and went out to light others and the light continues to dispel the darkness from the hearts of men all over the world.

CHAPTER XIII

¶ 136

The Poor

THERE was a militancy in the propaganda of Jesus when He championed the poor. In all periods of the Christian Era, His words were toned down, but at this distance of time they still cut like a rapier. None of His sayings have received such pruning, toning, and twisting as the saying, **'The poor ye have always with you.'** It has been almost universally interpreted to mean a justification of poverty. Parasites and exploiters in all times have used the saying as a cloak to cover their meanness.

A box of precious ointment had been broken and used to anoint Him. Some grateful heart found in that a way to show gratitude. There was a murmur about waste. A critic suggested that it might have been sold and the money given to the poor.

'Why trouble the woman,' He said, **'the poor you have with you always. Me you have not always with you.'**

This simple statement of fact has been interpreted to mean the announcement of a law of nature, or a dictum of God.

When He said it was as easy for a camel to go through the eye of a needle as for a rich man to enter the Kingdom of Heaven, the commentators enlarged the eye of the needle to the proportions of a wicket gate.

In one instance, responsibility for poverty is laid

by inference on the shoulders of the Almighty, and in the other, the difficulties encountered by the rich, in hanging on to all that is best and most comforting in both worlds, have been reduced to a negligible consideration.

Jesus had an affectionate regard for those who had reached the bedrock condition of human misery. If this is not clearly understood in the twentieth century, the upper classes made no mistake about it in the first He was stigmatised as a friend of the rabble   He was, and took no umbrage at being so considered.   The hungry multitude was to Him the ripe harvest of the Kingdom.

In His matchless picture of the great judgment, He identifies Himself with the poor, and delcares that a denial of the essentials of life, to His friends, is equivalent to a denial of the Father.   His 'good news' had an economic background.   His advocacy of the poor weakened the authority of the civil and religious exploiters.   The promulgation of new religious principles, or the rejuvenation of old ones, would have created no furore in Jerusalem, but a declaration of the right to bread was a disturbing factor.

The prevailing message of organised religion, at the beginning of the nineteenth century, was one of authority, obedience, gratitude for alms, and servile subordination.

The one thing dreaded in that day, was the inoculation of the English working man's mind with the sacramental phrases of the French Revolution.   At a time when one of every seven Englishmen was a pauper, Parliament voted a million pounds for the erection of Churches in which to preach submission to the superior classes.

Jails and gibbets, racks and tortures, magistrates, lay and clerical, with all the terror of the law, were not sufficient to keep the poor in order, so it was determined to make a larger use of religion, to enforce oppression.

The Pharisees of the early part of the nineteenth century took the same attitude toward the teachings of Jesus as the Pharisees of Jerusalem took, when they heard them from His lips. Had Jesus lived in England at the time, He would have been the friend of the factory slave, the defender of the little chimney sweeps, and the associate of all who groaned and suffered under the galling yoke of a civilisation that was called by His name.

Renan is far removed from the facts when He describes Jesus as loving poverty for poverty's sake. There never was and never could be any 'charm' attached to 'pious mendacity,' nor was it ever in the mind of the Master as a 'virtue.' Poverty is a curse. It always was, and will be as long as it exists. Lack of the essential food, clothing, and shelter turns man back into the animal condition of fang and beak and claw. It forces men to concentrate their minds exclusively on material things. The human soul that survives such condition, survives, not by virtue of poverty, but in spite of it.

If poverty was a virtue, why should Jesus castigate the rich for their exploitation? He loved the poor because He found they possessed the values that made more apt disciples in the Kingdom. They were simple-minded, humble-hearted, and open-souled. They could see more clearly the celestial vision. From the poor, therefore, He selected His apostles, His friends, and His intimate acquaintances.

¶ 137

The Sick

Jesus was not a mere medical missionary in Galilee, but He healed disease. His own appraisement on healing was not high. It was incidental. Physical distress was as real to Him as moral distress. Disease was largely a result of a low state of vitality, exacting toil, poor food, uncertainty, worry, care, and ignorance of life. Jesus had a genius for sympathy, and it was never better expressed than in healing disease. The blind and the lame and the tormented came to Him.

They professed no faith, they made no claims. He asked for none. To be in need of whatever He could give was the open door to relief.

The action of one mind upon another, which results in healing, has become so common, that it no longer excites wonder. Jesus, endowed with a personality that changed by mere contact the lives of men, was not hedged about by ordinary limitations. No genius ever is. He possessed the power and used it. So did His apostles later. The custodians of the truth in later years lost that power. What they lost, they denied others could possess, but with the extension of knowledge, the development of psychology, and a clearer vision of life and its meaning, have made us familiar with what, in the first century, seemed a setting aside of the laws of nature. As men realise their place in the scheme of things, the miracles of to-day become the commonplaces of to-morrow. To the distressed of body and mind, Jesus ministered. **'Come unto me, all ye that labour and are heavy laden, and I will give you rest,'** was an invitation of peculiar joy and relief to those afflicted with ailments of a bodily nature. There was no magic in the cures. It was a thought-writing of a divine personality on the mind of another. By the spoken word, by the power of suggestion, by an act of communion, the will of the Master acted upon the will of the recipient, and the body responded to the union of souls.

Personal contact was unnecessary then, as it is now. Distance mattered nothing. Thought waves travelled, and, as healing agencies, functioned in correlating and harmonising the body and spirit of man. He gave His apostles power to do likewise. He told them how, and in what condition, it could be done. He is doing that now, but no longer exclusively through those who bear His name.

'The healing of the sick,' says Renan, 'was considered one of the signs of the Kingdom of God, and was always associated with the emancipation of the poor.'

'Who would dare to say, that in many cases   .   .   .

the touch of a superior being is not equal to all the
resources of pharmacy? The mere pleasure of seeing
Him cures. He gives only a smile, or a hope, but these
are not in vain.'

There was a time when this statement of Renan
would have found no quarter in the scientific world.
To-day, the foremost scientists have left the timid
reasoner a long way behind. Psychology has opened
up new avenues of approach to the secret of soul power,
of which Jesus was the supreme manifestation.

In healing, He was no mere thaumaturgic or exorcist.
He healed at times in spite of Himself. It was His
intense sympathy with those in pain, that led Him to
ease the poor of their physical discomforts. It was a
phase of the great moral revolution, by which he raised
the proletariat to standing room on the continent of
the grace of God.

¶ 138

Victims

Israel's God was from time immemorial the defender
of the poor and oppressed.

Jesus was the champion of all classes of social and
ecclesiastical victims. If the Jewish law stood in the
way of doing good on the Sabbath, then Jesus came,
not to fulfil it but to smash it. When taken to task for
being natural on the Sabbath, He told the blind leaders
of the blind that the Sabbath was made for man, and
not man for the Sabbath.

The early Christians clung to the Jewish view of the
Sabbath, nevertheless, and organised Christianity of
the present day, despite the words of Jesus, takes the
same view. In some instances, the Christians out-
pharisee the Pharisees. Men were victims of a letter-
worship that excluded God. From this yoke of Sabbatic
bondage, Jesus relieved those who followed Him. To
those carried along on the ground swell of discontent, He

was ever a source of comfort. To men and women who suffered under a galling servitude of empty religious observances, He did not bring an equally burdensome network of abstruse creeds and doctrines. It was the condition of the human soul that sanctified or profaned the day.

The victims of hunger He fed: the victims of religious servility He emancipated: the heart-broken He relieved by a cure for care. Buddha offered a religion of deliverance from feeling, which was to rescue men from the pain of existence. Jesus recognised suffering as an inevitable element in life. He taught men how to bear it. He taught them by bearing it Himself. He touched life at every angle, and made Himself at one with the race.

He made no onslaught on money as such, but He emancipated the victim—such as Matthew Levi—who had tried and failed to find in it soul satisfaction.

If we are asked what His attitude toward work was, we reply that He was a carpenter. If we are asked why He made no attack on the Jewish idea of women, we recall the tender associations with Bethany, the conversations with women as with men. The claim that the improved status of women in the modern world is due wholly to Christianity is not valid. Many influences, having no connection with organised religion, have had a part in woman's emancipation. Women in old Japan and ancient Egypt had far superior status than they had under organised Christianity up to quite recent times. But the attitude of Jesus toward women was exactly as it was toward men. The followers of Jesus at no time, in the so-called Christian era, have followed His example. Millions of women in Christian countries have not yet arrived at the status possessed by women in ancient Egypt, where judicially she was the equal of man, and could dispose of her own property.

Even to the most degraded of women, Jesus showed a sympathy and tenderness that would be as startling now as it was then.

In the third decade of the twentieth century, we are

still debating whether women shall be given an equality with men in the Church, and the debate is likely to continue for many decades to come. Moses and Paul are our guides in this matter—not Jesus.

To Him, the human touch was more potent than law. Love is the supreme peacemaker. He would have us forgive our enemies, for they too are victims, and to return good for evil is the only way to their emancipation. **'Father, forgive them, for they know not what they do.'** In His thought-writing, He tried to produce in men the values He best exemplified in His own life.

I met a man once who reminded me of Jesus. He was considered a fool by his contemporaries. He was a doctor of medicine who inherited a million. He gave up his profession, and he gave the million to a board of trustees, to be administered for the use of the community in which the money was made. He made a legal transfer in such a way that he could never touch the money himself, nor have anything to say about its expenditure. He worked with his hands for a living, so that he might identify himself with the victims of an un-Christian social order. He goes from city to city, living in the cheapest lodgings, so that he may be one of the 'hobos' or tramps and help them by advice. He has no money to give. He gives himself—a fool for the Master's sake, throwing away his life, in order that he may find it.

This characteristic attitude of personal touch with the victims that still makes Jesus the wonder of the world we now delegate to slum missionaries and curates. The more eminent a man becomes in matters intellectual, the more honours, preferments, and emoluments he receives, the higher the walls that separate him from that personal touch with the sort of people of whom Jesus was the champion and personal friend.

¶ 139

Children

Just before His departure for Galilee some faithful ones brought their children to receive His blessing.

The disciples, probably getting ready for the journey, rebuked these parents, but Jesus said:—

'Suffer little children to come unto me, and forbid them not! for of such is the Kingdom of heaven. Truly I tell you, who will not receive the Kingdom of God as a little child, shall not enter therein!'

To this account Mark adds a touch—beautiful and characteristic: 'He took them in His arms and blessed them,' Matthew omits this but adds a 'child saying.' Just as His love for children has been a fruitful theme in art and literature for many centuries, it has furnished orators and preachers with inspiration—a shallow inspiration that ended very largely in words.

The century in which England revolutionised her methods of producing goods was a century of dishonour to English children.   It was a reign of terror, inhumanity, and savagery for the children of the poor.

The church had abandoned the guardianship of souls. She had become a mere cog in the new industrial machine. There were two theories of conduct toward the poor. One was that the spiritual equality of believers demanded a fair consideration for the weak, here and now. That theory was held by the few to whom the teachings of Jesus were still vital.   The other theory was that in the next world the poor would be recompensed for their miseries in this one.   That was the prevailing theory, overwhelmingly so, and had the sanction of the church. By virtue of that theory and under that sanction a species of barbarism was perpetrated on the children of the poor that would make savages blush.

The subjection of weak, underfed, and underclothed bodies to the overstrain of degrading physical exhaustion, was accompanied by mental starvation.   It was the belief of the governing classes that the less the poor knew the better they worked.   The right of a child to knowledge was denied.   Education bills for a hundred years were defeated by the leading statesmen of both political parties. 'Pass this Education Bill,' said one of the greatest statesmen of the nineteenth century, 'and you will make England a nation of infidels.'

A few zealous souls like Hannah More believed that the poor children should know the Bible in order that they might know something about God and Hannah More's God was a Deity who demanded obedience, gratitude, and order. So she organised classes and taught them the Book of Genesis.

We have made vast improvements in the last thirty or forty years, but we are yet a long way from an order of which Jesus could give His approval. In the cotton communities of the United States we still have the oppression of little children. We are still grinding profits out of them at a time when they should be attending school. The rise of the working class on both sides of the Atlantic brings us gradually nearer the ideals of the Master.

The barbarous treatment of the children of the poor by people of the English-speaking world, was not wholly due to the lust for gain. That had much to do with it, but the loving tenderness of Jesus towards children has been lost sight of. It has been smothered by the legalism of Moses and the theological doctrines of Paul.

No one has ever explained why Paul made but one solitary reference to the sayings of Jesus. The greatest defenders of the rights of little children are not infrequently considered enemies of both church and state.

'Let the children first be fed,' He said to the Syrophenician. 'And He called a little child unto Him and set him in the midst of them' as the type and pattern of the Kingdom. **'Whoso shall receive one such little child receiveth me,'** was one of His tests of genuine discipleship. It was so human, so tender, and full of charm.

CHAPTER XIV

MISSING THE MARK

¶ 140

It is unthinkable that Jesus made an outline of the doctrine of sin and left it to be filled in by Paul or John or Augustine or Calvin or Luther. In view of the tremendous emphasis laid upon this theme by these leaders it is remarkably significant that in all His teaching there are few traces of any abstract instruction on the question. In the first three Gospels the word sin occurs only about twenty-five times. In the rest of the New Testament it occurs 170 times. The difference is a matter of emphasis. The nearer men are to God the less they see of evil. It was said of God that His eyes were too pure to behold iniquity. The same was true of Jesus. He saw sin as the Father sees it. He treated it as the Father treats it. All the great leaders of the world, before and after Jesus saw in the nature of man a force that makes for uprighteousness. Platonic, Stoic, and Philonian philosophies conceived the spirit of man as originally divine, unsmirched and immortal. They believed that man possessed a power by which impure and sensual thought could be overcome. Paul made sin an intellectual abstraction, a theological concept. To him the sinful principle was an independent entity—an active subject to which any number of predicates might be attached. He regarded the natural condition of man as in universal subjugation to the bondage of sin and death; a fate brought upon the race by the sin of the first man Adam, imposed by divine decree and executed by demoniac powers.

205

Jesus only mentioned sin about a dozen times during the whole of His ministry, and when He did mention it, His attitude seems to have had more in common with the Greek conception than with the Hebrew. This seems all the more remarkable since Paul was in matters of the intellect an undoubted Hellenist.

Jesus never dogmatised on sin. He assumed it as He assumed the Father. He had clear distinctions between good and evil, right and wrong. If Adam's disobedience wrecked the human race and placed it under a curse to all eternity, Jesus never recognised the process. Nothing He ever said was more characteristic than that. He knew what was in man. He shared men's joy. He wept over their sorrows. He came to seek and save that which was lost. The lost were those who had wandered away from the Father. The religion of Jesus is based on what He taught. What He said of sin, therefore, must be as fundamental as what He said on love, or life, or religion.

Nor can we say that what He taught on the subject obtains its interpretative value in the light of subsequent history. On this as on all other topics He spoke as one having authority and not as the Scribes. If Jesus was the ultimate guide to God, He was the supreme authority on how to get there, and the chief obstacle in the way is sin The Greek word *Hamartia*, we translate sin. It means missing the mark. The tendency to shoot low or wide in morals, seems deeply embedded in human nature. John the Baptist harangued the multitude to change their minds. A literal translation of the word repent is: 'get another mind.' Jesus went deeper. He told them how to do it and how to sustain the change when they made it.

A low aim, therefore, was sin. In shooting at a target, from which the figure is taken, the hand and eye co-operate. In morals the call is to the will. Repentance is a change of mind—from a low aim to a high one, from an ignoble to a noble, from a selfish to an unselfish.

The ten commandments were all negative. They were legal deterrents which didn't deter. Jesus added to them. **'A new commandment I bring unto you**

—that ye love one another.' Love is positive, not negative, it is dynamic, not static. Wherever we find Jesus discoursing on sin, He is measuring men, not by the Law of Moses but by the law of God. When love failed to produce a new mind He did not fall back on the law of Moses to enforce His teaching. He never appealed to the State. His citizenship was of the Kingdom and His law was love.

One of the major charges brought against Jesus was that He fraternised with sinners. The charge was true. Those upon whom society had stamped its ban of disapproval were the recipients of His tenderest solicitude. He spoke in warm, tender accents to the woman taken in sin. He was quite at home amongst the nondescript guests at Matthew's feast. Men and women who had violated the law found in Him a friend. He saw the motive behind the overt act. Under the conditions in which the masses lived—exhaustive toil, scarcity of creature comforts, and small outlet for self-expression— the people were often goaded into rebellion and crime To such He presented the Kingdom, and with it His intimate fellowship.

With Paul sin is an intellectual abstraction—the keystone of a technological structure. Jesus does not appear to have taken that view. He knew the nature of the low aim and the power within that makes for evil, better than Paul knew it, yet He takes a different view. He makes deeper soundings. The moralist sees sin in action. Jesus sees it before it acts. He points out that the desire that only lacks opportunity is as culpable as the overt act. To a great crowd He said:—

'There is nothing without a man that entering into him can defile him: but the things that come out of him, those are they that defile the man.'

When He left the multitude and went into the house with His twelve friends they at once asked Him what He meant? Jesus gently rebuked the twelve for dullness.

'Are you without understanding also?'

That He was speaking of the things of the spirit had

not been quite plain to them. He explains that what goes in goes to the stomach. That which comes out comes from the heart—out of which come the issues of life.

'That which cometh out of the man, that defileth the man.' He explains how. Because the heart is the man—the real man. What He sends out is the essence of Himself.

'Out of the heart,' Jesus explains, 'proceed evil thoughts, adulteries, fornications, murders, thefts, covetousness, wickedness, deceit, lasciviousness, an evil eye, blasphemy, pride, foolishness. All these come from within and defile the man.'

How does the 'coming out' defile the man? Because the heart of every man is a chamber of imagery. When the natural heart is untouched by the divine, its imagery is of the self and the self life, and as he sends out his images whether in the form of words or thoughts, they reproduce themselves in the minds of others It is quite plain, therefore, that the man is defiled because he defiles others. Sin is anti-social. The process is like taking a picture from the wall of one room and hanging it in another. If a man's chamber is vulgar, his images are vulgar. Any one who has ever been forced to listen to a vulgar story knows that it takes many years to remove the picture from the mind Five centuries before Jesus came, Empedocles offered this prayer:—

'But O ye gods, turn aside
From my tongue
The madness of these men.
Hallow my lips.
And make a pure stream
Flow from them!
And thee, much-wooed,
White-armed Virgin Muse,
Do I beseech, that I may hear
What is lawful
For the children of a day!

Constrain me not to win garlands
Of honour and glory
At the hands of mortals
On condition of speaking
In my pride beyond that
Which is lawful and right,
And only so to gain a seat
Upon the heights of widsom!'

Evidently some undesirable pictures had been hung in the image gallery of the old Sicilian, and he prayed that he might have the power to prevent the reproduction of the 'madness.' Peter had a like experience, and the Master said, '**I have prayed the Father that you shall be preserved!**'

I was a labourer once in a pine forest. The workers were white men and negroes. At the close of the day, the darkness was lit up by blazing pine logs. Each race around its own fire. The colour line was sharply drawn. I sat with my race and listened to a foul, impure stream of the most vulgar stories. Fifty yards away sat the black men singing the songs of a slave race. The melody was weird but beautiful and reached out to a world beyond, where there are no slaves. The contrast was sharp. 'What comes out of a man' in the margin of the day usually reveals the pictures in his mind. What came out of the white men hurt—what came out of the black men helped. It was hard not to feel ashamed of one's race.

¶ 141

The Double-Minded

Jesus warned of the danger of hell, the impure of heart, the wilfully rebellious, the proud, arrogant religious leaders, the double-minded, the unstable who could not make up their minds and those who could not see him in His followers, however humble they might be. He did not define hell. He did not argue about it. His interpreters did. They defined it as a palce and enforced

their definitions, not as He would by the gentle persua-
sive power of love but by fire and sword and torture.

In the great charter He warns men of the results of
anger. Anger is sin. So is unfair judgment—so is
impure thought. All of these are the materials out of
which men forge the chains that bind their own souls
and the souls of others. They are the corrupt trees
that bear corrupt fruit. Better to pluck out an eye than
that it should continue to see only evil. Better to cut
off a hand than that it should be an offence. There is
no harangue against social crimes such as theft, or murder, or adultery. Anger is the womb in which murderous ideas are born. Covetousness is the mother of theft.
An impure eye is the image-maker of the sins that corrupt the flesh—and the image is the origin of the act.
Even the most intimate of His friends were so slow to
grasp His idea of the image, that He had to explain it
as if He were addressing children. Like their contemporaries, they were only concerned with the act. Jesus
taught them to examine the mental trail along which
the act travelled. He saw clearer than any of his interpreters have ever seen that men are more easily introduced into the Kingdom by conviction of righteousness
than by conviction of sin. It was so much easier to
enter the Kingdom of God by the persuasion of the
Master than it is to enter any sect by the door of a
creed.

'No man having put his hand to the plough and looking back.'

This type of mind might be a religious type, but it
fell short of His measurement for the Kingdom. This
is the type of man who sits on the fence. He cannot
make up his mind. He has one talent and buries it.
He knows what to do but he refuses to do it. He takes
hold of the handles of the plough and then looks back.
He has committed no overt act of sin. He has broken
no ecclesiastical law—but he is just short of the requirements, and as Jesus said, is unfit for the Kingdom. He
might make church material. He might have money
to give or prestige to raise the social tone, but for such

things Jesus cared nothing: they did not count. They count with us but our standards are not His standards

Judged by contemporary standards, the Pharisees were the strictest sect of the Jews; they were custodians of religion, leaders of thought, aristocrats of the temple area. The chief trouble with the Pharisees, ancient and modern, was a moral astigmatism. They were not able to discern the difference between a camel and a fly—spiritually. In spiritual values they were prone to put the wrong labels on the packages. They were almost as resentful of criticism as a modern churchman. Yet they themselves were sermon tasters and connoisseurs in all matters pertaining to religion. While the Master gave His tenderest sympathy to profligates and outcasts of all kinds and degrees, He had quite a different reception for the religious leaders Hypocrisy always aroused His gentle nature into a vehement storm of indignation. He attacked them with a scorn and contempt that made men marvel at His boldness. He attacked not because He harboured the slightest tinge of resentment, but because of the multitude who were there. For their sakes He gave an estimate of spiritual values. Just as He did in the house of Simon, when there were but a few present. The people were continually being fooled by the sophistries of the pseudo-religionists. Whenever Jesus entered into controversy with the Pharisees, the people saw at once the difference. Mere formal profession, then as now, blocked the way to God. Jesus undertakes to give real values. He calls things by their proper names. These professors had less religion than the profligates around them. They played and toyed with eternal verities They were sticklers for minute details of ceremonial observances, but the essence of religion which is love to God and love to one's neighbour they generally knew nothing about. Jesus strips the paint from the rotten cheek of religious hypocrisy and with keen penetrating irony shows the multitude that if they want to get to God they must brush these blockheads aside and open their hearts to the Father Himself. Like a thunderbolt

His words penetrated the hollow souls of the Pharisees and they slunk away, as they did who brought an accused woman to Him. No harlot ever shot so wide of the mark as did these custodians of the Temple. The morality of outcasts was infinitely higher than theirs. Jesus put a higher estimate upon their souls. They had less hypocrisy, they had fewer illusions. An illusion is something camouflaged. It is a superficial appearance that hides a reality. When the illusion is believed it becomes a delusion. The Pharisees had the outward show of religion but within they were empty and devoid of the essence.

Despite these judgments and values of Jesus in things spiritual we are still confronted with the Pharisee in religion. He is still measuring men by creeds and dogmas and ceremonies.

¶ 142

A Vision of Judgment

Jesus laid greater stress upon sins of omission than upon any other kind. He painted a word picture of a final judgment. It is a wonderful piece of imagery. We see the gathering of the nations of the world, we see the Son of Man in His glory and accompanying Him the hosts of heaven. It is a world festival of rejoicing and gladness. It is the great finality. Life's struggles are ended and the new era begins, but like life itself there is the inevitable note of sadness, a dark line in the spectrum. The Son of Man is not only King. He is judge also and judgment is as inevitable as love. He applies His winnowing fan and divides the host. On one side stands the King's friends and on the other His enemies—those who are crowned with blessing and those who are called accursed. Here is Matthew's account—arranged by Dr Briggs:—

I

When the Son of Man shall come in his glory, and all
    the angels with him,

Then shall he sit on the throne of his glory:
And before him will be gathered all the nations:
And he shall separate them one from another,
As the shepherd separateth the sheep from the goats:
And he shall set the sheep on his right hand, but the
    goats on his left.

II

Then shall the King say unto them on his right hand,
Come, ye blessed of my Father, inherit the Kingdom:
Which was prepared for you from the foundation of the
    world:
For I was an hungered and ye gave me meat: I was thirsty
    and ye gave me drink:
I was sick, and ye visited me: I was in prison, and ye
    came unto me.

III

Then shall the righteous answer him, Lord!
When saw we thee an hungered and fed thee, or athirst
    and gave thee drink?
When saw we thee a stranger, and took thee in, or naked
    and clothed thee?
When saw we thee sick and visited thee? or in prison and
    came unto thee?
And the King shall answer and say unto them, Verily
    I say unto you,
Inasmuch as ye did it unto one of the least of my brethren,
    ye did it unto me.

IV

Then shall the King say also unto them on the left hand,
Depart from me, ye cursed, into Gehenna,
Which is prepared for the Devil and his angels:
For I was an hungered and ye gave me no meat: I was
    thirsty and ye gave me no drink,

I was a stranger, and ye took me not in: naked, and
ye clothed me not:
I was sick, and ye visited me not: I was in prison, and
ye came not unto me.

V

Then shall the wicked answer him, Lord!
When saw we thee an hungered (and did not give thee
meat), or athirst and (gave thee not drink)?
(When saw we thee) a stranger (and took thee not in)
or naked (and clothed thee not)?
(When saw we thee) sick (and did not visit thee), or
in prison (and did not come unto thee)?
Then shall he answer and say unto them, Verily I say
unto you,
Inasmuch as ye did it not unto one of the least of these,
ye did it not to me!

The judgment scene is more of a parable than a
vision. The parallel truth is clear and unmistakable.
It is a pronunciamento on sin. The Son of Man at
earth's final wind-up asks no abstruse theological
questions. When the theologians come up for judgment they are astounded that their creeds and beliefs
and forms and ceremonies count for nothing—absolutely nothing. The final test is not what they
have believed, or imagined they believed. It is not a
question of what sect they choose, or whether they
were baptized by immersion or sprinkling—or whether
they believe that sin began with Adam or with themselves. Sin in this great preachment is lack of courtesy,
kindness, generosity, and love. And it was so simple,
so clear, and so easy of discernment that when the
records began to be written, many of the writers made
subtle attempts either to explain it away or at least
to make it seem more profound to the cultured of
Greece and Rome. It has never been incorporated
in any scholastic doctrine of sin. It has always occupied a secondary place. If God in anger at Adam

over the apple episode in the garden, declared that the human heart was naturally and inherently bad, Jesus does not seem to have known it. On the contrary, He assumed that good was fundamental and evil incidental. He took a little child and explained that it was the type of the Kingdom. When they asked whether the man who was born blind sinned or his parents, He said, **'Neither.'** The force He recognised as evil in man was of the same nature and essence as the force with which He contended in the wilderness. It was a low aim—and the low aim preferred the gratification of the desires of the body to the fulfilment of spiritual striving. It reduced men to a spiritually bankrupt condition. Jesus presented an ideal and urged men to strive for it. He asked them to strive for perfection,—**'Be ye therefore perfect even as your Father in heaven is perfect.'** Not to forgive one's enemies, not to be kind, not to be tolerant, not to be tender-hearted, not to be loving —all these were of sin. To postpone, procrastinate—to seek shelter in sophistry instead of the truth, was sin. When the Holiness of God was the incentive and men did not try to experience it *that* was missing the mark.

The teaching of Jesus on sin involves, includes, and incorporates a more profound psychology than the teaching of either Paul or John the Baptist, or any of the long succession of schools founded on their theology. It is devoid of fear or threat. The element of condemnation enters but only incidentally. He warns the ultra-religious hypocrites, but to all others He held up an ideal and urged men to reach it. He held up the idea of the good rather than wield a whip. He used a whip but that too was an incident. John's preaching was very powerful, very effective, but it lacked the love element that characterised the teaching of Jesus. The former urged men to get out of sin The latter told them how to get out and how to keep out. Darkness is the absence of light. One method urged men to expel the darkness. The other said, 'Get light, get plenty of light,' and the heart that is flooded with light will have no problem of darkness. One method is negative, the other is positive, one was denial, the other affirmation. The love, tenderness, and kindness of the Father is a greater incentive to pure living than threats of punishment or warnings of hell.

Jesus told the religious leaders of His day that they had substituted the traditions of men for the commandments of God, and that is exactly what has been done by modern teachers. He said they had shut up the Kingdom of Heaven and would neither go in themselves nor permit any one else to enter. He said they compassed sea and land to make one proselyte, and when he was made according to their tradition he became twofold more the child of hell than they were themselves.

He pointed out that it was the long-prayered, pious people who devoured widows' houses. These things are incidental to the main theological issues of to-day, but they were fundamental to Jesus. There was an intense prophetic severity in these utterances that the world is as much in need of now as it ever was.

Sin is centrifugal. It rusts and corrodes everything within the orbit of its influence. When He said to one who had missed the mark, **'thou art a stumbling block to me,'** He intimated that the offence had affected Him! Sins of omission are to us rather negligible values, but a careful study of His life shows conclusively that He laid greater stress on them than He did on active, deliberate, and overt acts of sin. To know the will of the Father and do it not was as much of a low aim, wide aim, at the mark as theft, adultery, or murder.

The mark we aim at is the Father's will. In doing that we aim high and sin is obviated by the active pursuit of the good. The lost are those who miss the mark and to such Jesus showed the way out—the way home to the Father, and no man has ever sincerely tried His method and failed.

CHAPTER XV

¶ 143

The Spirit of Gain

WHEN Jesus said men could not serve both God and mammon He was not delivering a pronunciamento against money or wealth. He was speaking of the form these things usually assume. Great wealth held in the possession of a single person becomes power. It might be a power for good, but it seldom is.

From the beginning of history the *spirit of gain* has been the chief obstacle to God-like life. It has been a power that enslaved men's bodies as well as their souls. It is a master passion that permeates from centre to circumference the affairs of men.

Mammon is the god of the world. He is the deity of the tilted scales, falsely evaluating morals, art, industry, and religion. There is no department of human life from which the evil spirit is excluded. Mammon confronted Jesus, he confronted the disciples, and He confronts us The most pathetic figure in the New Testament is the rich young ruler. Jesus saw that in all other respects he was good material, but the god of comfort, ease, and worldly power held him as in a vise. **'How hardly,'** Jesus said, **'shall they that have riches enter into the Kingdom of heaven.'**

In the book of James we have a picture of Mammon's power in the infant church Men well dressed and having the appearance of wealth were given front seats. Men who were poor were treated with scant courtesy.

What a departure from the spirit and teaching of the Master! Mammon is now the great god Success. Throughout the centuries he has been the chief ingredient in the poisonous atmosphere in which religion lingers, withers, and dies. In his false scales education is weighed. In the first place he holds fast in his grip the chief educational centres. Without his aid no child may enter the 'select' and 'exclusive' seats of learning. Inspired by Mammon some of the world's best statesmen have opposed the education of the poor. They have assumed that the less they knew the more work could be gotten out of them. The value they put upon it was not a personal evaluation. They were moved by the power behind them—the subtle invisible power of the worshippers in the temple of the god of gain.

The opposition to Jesus was largely prompted by the fact that He was the champion of the poor. He was made to feel the power of Mammon because to the apotheosis of lucre poverty was the cardinal sin.

The idea which made the Kingdom 'the antithesis of the world' was devoid of that which characterised earthly kingdoms. The Kingdom was a complete revolution in governmental ideas. It was a gigantic dream of a spiritual democracy in which money, land, heritage, and tangible appurtenances would cut no figure whatever.

The spirit that lusted for money and the things that money could procure: power, place, social distinction, and prestige, Jesus names, personifies, and makes stand out in bold relief as Mammon—the deification of wealth, which is the antithesis of God.

Mammon has many names. When he hoards we call him *avarice*. When he opens the flood gates of the lower self and becomes the incarnation of self-indulgence, we call him *sensuality*. When he talks loudly of what he is and what he has, we call him *egotism*. When he sets himself above the law and rides rough-shod over the rights of others, we call him *crime*

When his eyes are red and his hands are bloodstained; when armed and federated he marches through plunder, rapine, and death to conquest, we call him *war*. When he exalts brute cunning over the cardinal virtues, when he cracks the whip over the backs of factory children and exploits for his personal advantage the lives of men, when he lies and cheats in weights and measures and accounts and schedules, when in business he acts on the principle of 'live I, die you,' we call him *trade*.

Mammon is not only the god of gain, he is also the god of success and respectability. He works for glory and despises the inglorious. He is success, and metes no mercy to the unsuccessful He leads the social whirl, he sits in the front pew. He makes laws to protect his interests. He stands beside the publisher, the author, the artist, the legislator, and the clergyman. He asks but the question—'Does it pay?' Everything to him has but one value—a cash value. He is the exalted guardian of vested rights. He is the arch defender of things as they are. He is prudent, careful, and sane. To him the Kingdom of God is a myth, and disinterested love a chimera. He laughed at Jesus, he laughs at us. He is called 'practical' and 'hard-headed.' To him virtue is something that can be cashed in the coin of the realm.

'Ye cannot serve God and Mammon,' is no mere catch phrase. It is a statement of eternal truth. Blessed are the poor, for they have nothing that Mammon can get a grip on. Blessed are ye humble, for ye are not tempted by the subtle allurements of social distinction. Blessed are ye that are hungry, for ye have not been corrupted by food that belonged to others. Blessed are ye that are persecuted, for God is your champion.

¶ 144

The Respectability of Mammon

If the Mammon of Jesus' day whipped the world with whips—the Mammon of our day lashes us with scorpions. Religion is freer and more widespread, but Mammon is more deeply embedded in life. Mammon has become ultra-respectable. To many religious people he is God's silent partner. He preaches thrift for the poor. The pecuniary virtues have become cardinal. He is benevolent and gives of his surplus to those who do not worship in his temple. He is patriotic and believes that all is fair in war and business. He is a patron of art and learning. He transmutes the blood of the workers into marble halls, cathedrals, and universities. All his writings are piously phrased All his public acts are marked by decorum and order. He quotes scripture, and one of his favourite tests is.—

'The poor ye have always with you.'

The spirit of Mammon and the spirit of the Master are as far asunder as the poles. They are in conflict. They are diametrically opposed to each other and cannot remain equal tenants of the same heart. Jesus said that the meek would inherit the earth. Mammon disputes the claim. He urges the successful and the strong to hold all they have and take all they can get. Jesus says,—

'A man's life consisteth not in the abundance of the things which he possesseth.'

Mammon says it does, and points out that only those abundantly blessed in goods receive social recognition.

'Foxes have holes, and the birds of the air have nests, but the Son of Man hath no where to lay his head.'

Mammon says it is a question of efficiency, frugality, and thrift. He names great men who began low down in the scale of possession and amassed great fortunes. Mammon has not only made the possession of great accumulations respectable but he has added his benediction to the process. The early church tried communism. Mammon pointed out the foolishness of the venture, and introduced the competitive system—which is war in industry. There the battle is to the strong and the race to the swift, and the weak and slow are gathered together and cast into the Gehenna of modern industrial methods. There is a humourous aspect to all this. It has the blessed sanction of the friends of Jesus. In the peasants' revolt, when the overlords slaughtered a hundred thousand labourers, Luther was Mammon's chief defender. He said that a prince could get to heaven as easily by slaughtering peasants as by prayer. His chief literary contribution to this bacchanalia of the god Success was a pamphlet entitled, *Against the murderous thieving hordes of Peasants.*

'A rebel,' said the great theologian and son of a miner, 'is outlawed of God and Kaiser. Therefore who can and will first slaughter such a man, does right well, since upon such a common rebel every man is alike judge and executioner. Therefore who can, shall here openly or secretly smite, slaughter, and stab; and hold that there is nothing more poisonous, more harmful, more devilish, than a rebellious man!' His advice was taken and religiously followed even to peasants of Belgium in 1914.

The peasants asked for 'Divine Justice.' They imagined a great theologian would understand that. Luther replied that the Gospel only guaranteed a spiritual and not a temporal emancipation. The result was that the peasants totally rejected Luther's kind of God—the god he preached to them was Mammon. The workers, the world over, with penetration and instinctive insight, detect the difference. When they hear this kind of preaching or any of its variants, they say: 'Sirs, we would see Jesus!' In front of me as I write there are three ponderous volumes—a commentary on the New Testament. They were written by Dr Ellicott, Bishop of Gloucester, a learned leader of the Church of England. When this interpreter of Jesus came in contact—not with a peasant revolt, but with an effort of labourers to organise themselves, he did not advocate murder, but he did say that the horsepond was a fitting destination for the 'labour agitators.'

That was about as far as civilised society in England would permit him to go.

When thousands of young ministers have received

from Luther and Ellicott their knowledge of Jesus, instead of from the Gospels, little is to be expected. The knowledge of Jesus held by both men was tempered by the *status quo*. It was not indifferent to the god of gain. There was a little of the spirit of Jesus, a good deal of the theology of Paul, and considerable bowing in the house of Rimmon!

The long laboured attempt of Mammon to 'modernise' Jesus has not met with much success. Mammon has succeeded, however, in changing the outward aspects of the Kingdom. In Galilee the Kingdom was proclaimed without money—or books, or newspapers, or, social prestige. It began as a simple heart to heart, mouth to ear, and hand to hand movement. It got along without the patronage of rich men. Its warm, congenial, democratic atmosphere was not a place in which to grow rich or exercise authority, or bestow dignity. The founder openly fought hypocrisy. He opposed the purse-proud as well as the proud of heart. He emphasised wealth of heart, but He knew from his own experience amongst men that other kinds of wealth came not by honest labour but largely by oppression and trickery and deceit. He was not a hater of wealth as such. He was a hater of the methods by which wealth was acquired.

The craze for riches was just as great then as it is now, but the opportunities were fewer. With Jesus it was not a matter of comfort or lack of comfort. He would not have despised a home of His own in Capernaum if conditions had been such that He could have had one in the spirit of the Kingdom. It was a matter of emphasis. Mammon was opposed to the simplicity of life as Jesus lived it. He moved the disciples to ask the Master what they were going to get out of following Him. He whispered in the ear of the young ruler and persuaded him to turn away. He whispered to Matthew Levi, but Matthew threw the shekels aside and chose the life spiritual.

The appeal to the flesh is insidious. And as the inner light burns low and enthusiasm wanes, the desire

for substitutes grows stronger.   The early church laid
more stress upon the theology of Paul than upon the
doctrine of the Kingdom, but they held fast to the spirit
of Jesus in the defence of the poor.

¶ 145

Mammon Unchanged

As organised Christianity departed from the simplicity of the Master and Christians assumed lordship
over one another in religious degrees and titles, they
gradually reached the stage of costly buildings, costly
furnishings, and costly living.   There have been many
revolts against this tendency.   Francis of Assisi em-
bodied in his crusade much of the fine sincerity and
simplicity of the Gospels.   The Wesleyan movement
of more recent times was another attempt to gather into
the Kingdom the poor, the workers, and the social types
that Jesus gathered around Him in Galilee.   Neither
the followers of Francis nor the followers of Wesley
have been able to maintain the high spiritual standards
of their founders.   What happened to one happened to
all.   The rich and well-to-do took possession and are
in possession now.   Where Mammon enters he corrupts.
The demand for money becomes intense and continuous.
Great buildings and great institutions require great
exchequers.   To these the poor and the toilers can contribute little.   Doves are not sold in the temples, money-
changing is done in business centres, but the money-
changers and the exploiters are the rulers of the synagogues and the toilers are not found there.   The whole
arrangement, while foreign to the ideas of Jesus, is quite
respectable, quite moral, quite æsthetic, quite proper, but
obviously quite unlike primitive Christianity.

The power of Mammon to poison a spiritual atmosphere is just about as it was in the first century.   Few
people wholly escape the conflict.   The power is subtle,
insidious, and deceptive.   Millions are unconscious
that they are under the spell of it.   They think in bulk.

Who, being a god, would not rather taint millions with pennies than dozens with millions? No, it is not the amount It is the spirit, the kind of spirit manifested in getting and holding the amount. God says, **Give;** Mammon says, Get. Both are right. It is the motive and purpose behind getting and giving that makes the difference.

CHAPTER XVI

CONSPIRACY AND MURDER

¶ 146

The Beginning of the End

To speak of the 'execution' of Jesus is to suggest a legal process. There was no legal process. He was lynched as the result of a conspiracy. His arrest by an armed mob was the first of a series of illegal acts.

Of the golden chain of intimate friends, the first link to snap was Judas. Nothing so acutely pains the human heart as the treachery of an intimate and trusted friend. Nothing so blights the soul as the rejection of disinterested love. The Master's rebuke was mild but explicit. Judas betrayed Him with a kiss and disappeared. The mob with torches, staves, and swords, advanced.

'Whom seek ye?' He asked.

'Jesus of Nazareth,' they said.

'I am He.'

Something in the tone of His voice, something in the look in His eyes, unnerved the rabble, and they shrank back.

'Whom seek ye?' He repeated.

'Jesus of Nazareth.'

'I have told you that I am He. If therefore ye seek me, let these go their way.'

The brute courage returned and they laid hands on Him. Peter, seizing a sword, made a smash at the nearest of the rabble, who happened to be Malchus, a servant of the High Priest. The blow deprived him

225

of an ear. Resistance ended there. Jesus surrendered Himself into their hands and they led Him away.

His first arraignment was before Annas—a former high priest—who assumed authority on the slender thread spun out of the fact that he was the father of Caiaphas's wife. He had no more legal right to try Jesus than the mob had to arrest Him. Annas perhaps was one of the informers. With the other dignitaries he wanted possession of Jesus in order to hand him over to Rome. It was a savage and fanatical vendetta, unscrupulous and illegal.

The session before Annas was brief. Caiaphas was present. Questions were put.

'I spoke openly to the world,' He said, **'I ever taught in the synagogues and in the temple, whither all the Jews come together, and in secret spake I nothing. Why askest thou me? Ask them which heard me, what I have said unto them. Behold they know what I said.'**

Many details are lacking in the narrative. His answer to one question displeased a flunkey and He was struck on the mouth. His answer to the man who struck Him was:—

'If I have spoken evil, bear witness of the evil, but if well, why smitest thou me?'

John and Peter were present. For some reason, unknown to us, John was admitted, but Peter was questioned. John spoke to the portress and Peter was admitted. At the fire, as he warmed himself, he was challenged again. Despite the warning of the Master, Peter had not sufficiently fortified himself. In a moment of zeal and indignation he drew the sword, but by the fire he stoutly denied his discipleship. When the cock crew, he remembered the warning and went out and wept bitterly.

From the first stage of the great farce before Annas, they conveyed Him across the courtyard to confront Caiaphas, the high priest. The second stage was also brief. From Caiaphas He was taken before the Sanhedrin. Of the proceedings there no record seems to have been made. They met at night, and as the case involved the life of the accused, the meeting at night was incontrovertibly illegal. There were false witnesses whose testimony was inaccurate and contradictory. Even the testimony of the Evangelists on what happened leaves much to be desired. Legal forms were utterly abandoned. Everybody seemed bent on His death. They were in a hurry to despatch Him. To-morrow might be too late. The multitude might take the law into their own hands and frustrate the designs of the officials. They were terror-stricken lest He should escape. It was now or never.

Sedition and blasphemy were the two charges. To say He was 'tried' on these charges would be a travesty on words. He was *accused* on them and condemned. Where was Nicodemus? If present he was a silent partner in the guilt of his friends. Where were the disciples? We can account for three, two of whom were in moral collapse.

'Art Thou the Son of God?' He was asked, and He answered, **'Ye say that I am.'** This to His accusers constituted the crime of blasphemy. Yet these sticklers for form knew that no man could be put to death either on the testimony of one witness or on his own alone. The first charge was untrue, the second was unjust   Yet He was pronounced worthy of death. The verdict was unanimous.

The sole authority in Judæa who had power of life and death in his Hands was not Annas, not Caiaphas, not the Sanhedrin, but the Roman Procurator, Pontius Pilate. The *jus gladii*, or right of capital punishment, was the principal attribute of Roman sovereignty. It was never under any circumstances relinquished. Writers of Christian history and leading men of the Church throughout its history have considered the assassination of Jesus 'unjust but not illegal.' As a background for certain theological dogmas this false belief served a purpose. The contemporaries of Irenæus and Tertullian lavished praise on Judas because by his base betrayal he facilitated the sacrifice of his Master.

¶ 147

Before Pilate

From the Sanhedrin they took Him to the Prætorium.
Jesus entered to confront Pilate, but His accusers
remained outside. Their hatred of their victim was
cooled somewhat by fear of Levitical contamination.
As they stand outside straining at the gnats of ecclesiastical convention and swallowing whole the camels
of hatred and murder, we must not think that they
monopolised that sort of thing. Thousands of just such
crowds with just such minds have harassed and persecuted and murdered and they have done it in the name
of the Nazarene who stood before Pilate.

The bandying of words between Pilate and the
rabble is interesting and brings out the character of
both. Not once is the sentence mentioned. It seems
to have been understood.

'What accusation bring ye against this man?' Pilate
asks.

'If this man were not an evildoer, we should not
have delivered him up unto thee.'

'Take him yourselves and judge him according to
your law.'

'It is not lawful for us to put any man to death.'

Nor was it lawful to pronounce sentence of death,
nor to condemn on the testimony of informers, nor
on testimony of the accused, nor to meet at night,
nor to execute sentence on the same day sentence was
delivered, nor even to arrest without authority in a
capital case. From the brutal assault in the garden
until they nailed Him to the Cross, every stage in the
conspiracy, every move in the faked trial, was a violation
of law. The sentence was, in the first place, illegal,
and, in the second place, unjust.

The dialogue between the world's supreme gentleman
and the truckling flunkey of bloodthirsty Rome is
interesting :—

'Art thou a king then?'

'**Sayest thou this thing of thyself,**' answered Jesus, '**or did others tell thee of me?**' He had no need, no desire to hedge. If the question was Roman, No; if from the Jews, Yes.

'Am I a Jew?' said Pilate, 'Thine own nation and the chief priests delivered Thee unto me. What hast Thou done?'

'**My kingdom is not of this world,**' Jesus answered; '**if my kingdom were of this world, then would my servants fight, that I should not be delivered to the Jews; but now is my kingdom not from hence.**'

A King, yes, of a spiritual Kingdom of God, a Kingdom He had proclaimed openly to the world.

'**Every one that is of the truth heareth my voice,**' said Jesus, and Pilate asked:—

'What is truth?'

Without waiting for an answer he went outside and said to the rabble, 'I find no crime in Him.'

The irresolute, vacillating procurator saw a loophole of escape from his dilemma. Jesus was a Galilean. Herod was regent of that province, and forthwith he sent the accused to Herod. Before that lecher Jesus open His mouth not at all! He was ridiculed, insulted, taunted, and, clad in white, as a further humiliation, was returned to Pilate.

'Ye brought unto me this man,' said Pilate to the accusers, 'as one that perverteth the people; and behold I, having examined him before you, find no fault in him touching the things whereof ye accuse him, no, nor yet Herod; for he sent him back unto us; and behold, nothing worthy of death hath been done by him. I will therefore chastise him and release him.'

Why chastise Him if no crime could be found in Him? There was no attempt to discover or discuss a single proof of His guilt. Pilate might just as well have said, 'He is innocent, but to please you I will whip Him!' Herein lies the cowardice of the procurator. He held the power of exoneration and release in his hands, but instead of using that power, threw the responsibility back on the infuriated mob.

¶ 148

The Mob Mind

'Now at that feast the Governor was wont to release unto the people a prisoner, whom they would. And they had then a notable prisoner, called Barabbas. Therefore when they were gathered together Pilate said unto them, Whom will ye that I release unto you? Barabbas or Jesus which is called Christ?'

Pilate had no desire to save Jesus. If he had, he never would have given the mob any choice. He would not have wavered before them. He knew enough about the mass mind to know that to have two opinions before such a solid concentrated mass of envy meant to that mob weakness and only weakness. He must have known the bent of that fury. It was bent on murder. He played with it, toyed with it. His wife seems to have had some conscience. He had none.

Three things held intact the mob madness: the evident vacillating weakness of the Procurator, the powerful suggestions of the chief priests, and the mob consciousness that it was evidently winning out. The weakest minds in the crowd had become strong, and the strongest had become weak. Mind became fused in mind. The minds had become a mind and the mind cried 'Crucify Him!' Everything Pilate did, every time he opened his mouth or waved a hand, he made more compact and added to the fury of that mass mind.

A crowd may be beaten or cowed by a strong personality if the crowd be, as this one, in the wrong. Even a mediocre mind in the position of authority such as Pilate held, might have thrown them back on their history, their laws, their prophets, or their literature. All of these were the greatest in history, and by their injustice and madness they were throwing them into the scrap-heap.

There was a hollow mockery in the cry, 'We have no king but Cæsar.' Pilate was not blind to its hypocrisy. If he had really desired to deal justly with the prisoner he would instantly have replied, 'Then as your King's representative I shall deal with the accused as you would have me deal with you.' If he had had any stamina, any courage, any conscience, that was the moment to hold the balance level. But the moment of opportunity passed. In a twinkling it was gone, for ever.

He called for water and went through the theatrical ceremony of washing his hands of the guilt of the accused and of the accusers. It was a vain show and deceived nobody.

Where at that moment were the throngs who had hailed Him as deliverer? Where were the thousands who had followed Him and hung on His words? Where were the Friends of that sacred circle? Not a single voice was raised in protest, not a friendly face was to be seen. The poor He had befriended, the rich He had healed, the heartbroken He had comforted —where were they? Why were they silent?

> 'The People is a beast of muddy brain
> That knows not its own strength
> And therefore stands
> Loaded with wood and stone:
> The powerless hands
> Of a mere child guide it with bit
>   And rein;
> One kick would be enough to break
>   the chain,
> But the beast fears
> And what the child demands
>   It does;
> Nor its own terror understands,
> Confused and stupefied by bugbears vain.
> Most wonderful! With its own hand
> It ties and gags itself;
> Gives itself death and war

For pence doled out by kings
From its own store.

Its own are all things
    Between earth and heaven;
But this it knows not,
And if one arise to tell this truth
    It kills him unforgiven.'

So wrote Campanella, in the light of the facts surrounding another martyrdom in the fifteenth century.
There is little to choose between the hatred, bitterness,
and murder in the hearts of the crowd that burned to
ashes the body of Savanorola and the ethics of the mob
that murdered Jesus. One was a Christian mob, the
other a mob of Jews. One had the light of fourteen
centuries of His gospel, the other had but a few years.
Both were murdered in the name of religion. The
Florentine mob was as devoid of reason, religion, and
humanity as was the mob in Jerusalem. Cardinal
Romolino was as weak, corrupt, and cowardly as Pilate.
Between them there is little to choose. Florence, though
as guilty as Sodom, survived. The Jews were scattered
to the four corners of the earth, and Rome fell with a
crash! It is said that the Florentines shuddered at the
cruel death of their prophet. Only the rocks of Golgotha
shuddered at the death of Jesus.

¶ 149

Behold the Man!

Pilate had Jesus scourged. Then He was arrayed
in a purple garment and a crown of thorns placed on
His head. When brutal whips had done their work
and the effort to humiliate and degrade was complete,
the Procurator pronounced the epilogue to the proceedings. Pointing to the Master, he said: 'Behold
the man!' The effect was a spontaneous outburst of

vindictive wrath.   It was like throwing a piece of meat to hungry lions in a cage.

'Crucify him! Crucify him!' they shouted.   More equivocation, more useless questionings, more shoutings for revenge, for execution, and the cowardly master of subterfuge released unto them the murderer Barabbas and handed over the stainless Galilean to the fury of his enemies.

There are variations in the accounts.   There are matters of detail that matter little.   What difference does it make when they flogged Him, or spat upon Him, or clothed Him in white or purple?   The sequence of savage events is of little interest.

It is of importance to observe, however, that this outrage occurred when the genius of Rome as a law-maker was at the very acme of its world-wide fame.

The entrance of Roman soldiers denoted the end of the farce, and Jesus was led away—away to the death of a criminal, without being tried either by Roman or Jewish law and in direct and flagrant violation of both.

The procession was a mixed multitude, a hetero-geneous mass of priests and soldiers, men, women, and children, Jews and Gentiles—scoffing, hooting, and jeering.   When the weight of the heavy ugly cross began to weaken the Master, there was not a man in the crowd who would lend a hand.   As a rift in the dark cloud it would be comforting to know that Simon of Cyrene had volunteered, but Matthew tells us that the soldiers commandeered him and forced him to carry it, as Jesus was no longer able.

The two thieves were evidently robust rogues and needed no assistance.   The commandeering of Simon is the first hint we get of the form of death to be met. Crucifixion was a Roman method   When Rome finally quelled the slave revolt under Spartacus, the victors spiked six thousand slaves to as many crosses and left them standing along the roadsides, as symbols of her power over life.   Slave-masters carried these ugly gibbets as part of their equipment.   The slave business furnished the largest number of victims of the extreme penalty and to the death of a slave as much humiliation and degradation as possible was always attached.

At Golgotha the victims were spiked to the wood and the crosses were erected. Perhaps it was merely fortuitous, but Jesus was put in the centre, between the two thieves. That was the place He would have chosen. By the stupid, the exploiter, and the oppressor, however religious, respectable, or socially circumstanced, sympathy with suffering has always been considered collusion with crime. He was 'numbered with the transgressors.' He was of the very texture of the social group called the people of the ground. We are just now beginning to understand that as a leader, a political leader, of the poor, He was more feared than as an innovator in religion.

The superscription over His head was in Hebrew, Greek, and Latin:—

'JESUS OF NAZARETH, KING OF THE JEWS'

He probably had that hanging about His neck all the way. The Jews wished to alter it, but Pilate decreed that it should remain as it was, and it remained.

Let us see who are there now, to whom He may cast a loving glance in the bitterness of His martyrdom. There were Mary Magdalene, Mary the wife of Cleopas, Salome the mother of John, Joanna the wife of Chusa, John, and Mary the Master's mother.

As in His life, so in the throes of death He manifested that strange mingling of the Divine and Human. His sympathy with His fellow-victim, His care for His mother as He committed her to the care of John, and His **'Father, forgive them, for they know not what they do.'** His tenderest thought was not alone for those who loved Him, but for the violent, misguided mob.

How all the past must have crowded the mind of His mother! All the countless incidents of those thirty years of obscurity when she alone knew of His visions, His ideals, His hopes. How meagre the records are in the things we would like to know. We are told what the rabble said. We know the soldiers cast lots for His garments, but of what His mother said or of what she was thinking, not a word.

Nor are we quite clear in our minds about the nature of the agony that brought to His lips the opening words of Psalm XXII. Taht also may be of minor consequence. What the thinking world will reject, however, is the theory that the Father's plan was accomplished by fraud, injustice, cupidity, falsehood, and murder. Spiritual superstructures built on that foundation have failed, always will fail, and ought to fail.

When the crushing weight of Jewish and Roman hatred fell upon Him, He bore it with fortitude and divine resignation, and while He prayed for His enemies He was evidently conscious that He was being foully assassinated.

To such a life there is no death. There is a change, a transition, the temple crumbles, disintegrates, and falls; the spiritual occupant bursts the limitations of the flesh and becomes free.

At the Third hour He belonged to the ages.

The incident of the cross manifested neither the contempt of the Greeks nor the dread of the Jews for what they called death. It was a human incident divinely faced. To the disciples and followers who were scattered and in hiding it seemed at the time the end of all things. It was really the beginning of all things. An old age passed out. A new age was ushered in. The hopes they entertained of political and material domination fell to the ground. But new hopes of a spiritual empire that would capture the hearts of mankind arose and took their places.

¶ 150

The First Easter Morn

'The idea of His life shall sweetly creep
Into their study of Imagination,
And every lovely organ of His life
Shall come apparell'd in more precious habit,
More moving—delicate and full of life,
Into the eye and prospect of their souls
Than when He lived indeed.'

The Master returned. He appeared to the fear-stricken Friends. His presence in the spirit inspired them with new life. It gave them a super power that burned in their hearts like a flame of fire.

We are still debating whether He came back in a broken physical body or in an astral body of a purely spiritual nature. The majority of people enrolled in the churches of organised Christianity seem to cling to the theory of a physical resurrection. If it is not insisted upon in the creeds, it is thundered from the pulpits that the immortality of the soul is conditional on the reanimation of the body in a physical resurrection. The theory of the physical corporeality of the person of the returned Master is probably based on the request for food and the invitation to handle, given in Luke XXIV. Paul's thesis on the resurrection is the greatest in Christian literature. The Gospels were not in existence when Paul wrote, but he does not appear to have ever heard the story or tradition mentioned by Luke.

The Master did not walk out of the tomb on Easter morning. He was never in it. Nor can we say literally that He 'returned,' for He had never been away. He was hidden from His friends, hidden and obscured by their doubts and fears and cowardice. Having the root of the matter in them, these things were passing clouds on a spiritual sky. When He appeared they realised the reality of things invisible, they became possessed of evidence of things not seen. Death having no terror

for Him, had no longer any for them.   The integuments
of illusion perished at the first meeting of the reunited
friends and the passion for righteousness had a new birth.

While Jesus was with them in the flesh the disciples
were mere children in the faith.   A few hours before
His arrest they were bickering about place and pre-
eminence in the Kingdom.   Despite His constant companionship and incessant teaching they did not seem to
grasp the full meaning of His mission.   Surpassing
as was the greatness of His personal influence before the
cross, it paled into insignificance when compared to the
power of His return from the shadow of death.

The record of the psychical experiences or spiritual
visitations is scant, and what He said seems little different
from what He had said already while with them in Capernaum.   Yet the effect was different—different and
immeasurably greater.   Under the spell of the new
impulse this handful of unlettered men went out to conquer the Roman Empire for the Kingdom of God.

The fervour and heat of the new evangel became
irresistible.   It broke the shell of its Judaistic origin,
and pressed out and beyond the frontiers of the Fathers
into the remote corners of the earth.   With hearts
aflame and tongues tipped with ineffable tenderness,
these working-class ambassadors of light preached and exemplified the religion of the pure heart and the open hand.

It is not too much to say that this divine enthusiasm
immediately following the Resurrection was the vessel
destined by the Father to preserve to the world the
religion of Jesus.

Violent reactions set in later.   The first apostles
had hardly passed away before sacerdotalism made its
appearance.   Then out of the infant church grew a
book, and out of the book grew an intricate network
of dogmas.   In the course of time we had an infallible
book, an infallible church, and an infallible head of a
large section of the church.   Out of these grew an authority and a discipline which in the course of centuries were
responsible for more bloodshed, cruelty, and perversion
than was ever laid to the charge of the Sanhedrin at
Jerusalem.

¶ 151

Hope for the Future

'The time cometh that whosoever killeth you will think that he doeth God service. And these things will they do unto you, because they have not known the Father, nor me.'

The custodians of the faith, blind and ignorant, not only did not know Him or His Father, but they were determined that the great mass of the people should remain ignorant even of the New Testament records.

'If God spare my life,' said William Tyndale, the father of the English Bible, to a priestly antagonist, 'ere many years I will cause a boy that driveth the plough to know more of the Scriptures than thou doest!' And he did, but it cost him his life. He was forced to fly from England in order to do it The English New Testament was born in Cologne in the year 1525. In 1536 Tyndale was strangled at the stake and his body burned to ashes. His dying words were, 'Lord, open the King of England's eyes.'

His New Testament was publicly burned at Paul's Cross, and the more they burned the larger grew the editions. A chronicler of that day named Hall gives this quaint description of a bishop's zeal: 'The Bishop, thinking he had God by the toe, when indeed he had the devil by the fist, said, "Gentle Mr Packington" (Packington had volunteered to buy up copies for him to burn), "do you diligence and get them; and with all my heart I will pay for them whatsoever they cost you, for the books are erroneous and naught, and I intend certainly to destroy them all and to burn them at Paul's Cross." Packington came to William Tyndale and said, "William, I know that thou art a poor man, and hast a heap of New Testaments and books by thee, for the which

thou hast endangered thy friends and beggared thyself."
"Who is the merchant?" asked Tyndale. "The Bishop
of London," said Packington. "Oh, that is because
he will burn them," said Tyndale. "Yea, marry,"
said Packington. "I am the gladder," said Tyndale,
"for these two benefits shall come thereof: I shall get
money to bring myself out of debt and the whole world
will cry out against the burning of God's Word; and the
overplus of the money that shall remain to me shall make
me more studious to correct the said New Testament and
so newly to imprint the same once again, and I trust the
second will much better like you than ever did the first."
And so forward went the bargain, the Bishop had the
books, Packington had the thanks, and Tyndale had the
money.'

The right to print and the right to read were secured
at great cost and took centuries to accomplish. The
right to think and the right to interpret made slower
progress. Many of the staintliest lives that ever
graced this earth were given in the effort to reduce the
high cost of thinking.

Bloodshed and the more violent forms of persecution
are no longer permissible, but a sort of spiritual hierarchy
still posts its sentries at the gates of heaven to keep out
Tyndale's ploughboys who have equal rights to read
but unequal rights to think and interpret.

These sentinels wear the livery not alone of one
dominant sect but of all sects. They are all equally
dogmatic and equally insistent upon dogmas. There
can be no religion without dogma, but, strange as it
may appear in the twentieth century, the one great
dogma of Jesus—the Kingdom of God—is a cancelled
passport!

Nevertheless, the situation is full of hope. The
sects are becoming courteous amongst themselves.
An eminent Christian minister of a small sect has been
permitted by an act of courtesy to preach in a cathedral!
That is the sensational incident of the day. It is unique,
and perhaps illegal, but full of hope.

In all sections of divided Christendom there are

men and women of light and leading, prophets, priests, and thinkers, who are re-thinking Jesus. They are exploring the vast continent of the human soul. They are digging, out of the rubbish of ages, the great big fundamental things that Jesus taught. A few more centuries and the world will reap what is being sown and the Saviour of the World will come into His own. On the shoulders of these torch-bearers there rests as great a responsibility as that which rested on the shoulders of the circle of intimate Friends at Capernaum.

CHAPTER XVII

¶ 152

The Theology of Jesus

THE theologians locked the truth up in words. They imprisoned it. Jesus appealed to the imagination. His images were windows through which all men could see God. He himself was God's word—the express *image* of His Person. He called His followers Friends. This Friendship was based on love, love to the Father and to each other. Love is the earth and moisture and sunshine that give life to the plant of discipleship. He did not call men to believe in a book. Life cannot be measured by a book. Life can be measured only by life. He did not call men to belief in miracles, or prophesies, or hells, or heavens, or ecclesiastical organisations. One may believe all these things and yet miss the main thing. He did not call men to a belief in Paul or Luther or Calvin, or the creeds they formulated. One may believe all these men taught and yet not be His friend or disciple. He called men to a belief in the Father and in each other, and in Him.

God as Father was the Alpha and Omega of the theology of Jesus. It was His 'body of divinity.' The poetry, sweetness, and charm of the word Father as Jesus pronounced it, arrested the attention of men. There was nothing of affection or familiarity in current forms of worship. To most men Jehovah was a benevolent despot. He was removed from the affairs of men. Jesus made Him familiar, He brought Him near. When the Jews in Old Testament times spoke of God as Father it had an official ring. Isaiah speaks of 'the mighty God, the Everlasting Father.' He was conceived as a jealous God who could laugh at calamity and mock when the heart was filled with fear. Wrath and judgment and terror were associated with His name. He was the God of the nation and could be approached through priests and ceremonies and sacrifices. He sat on a throne, and thrones are far removed from the common affairs of common people. If Jesus had been a theologian He would have removed God still farther from our personal sight and reach by definitions and disquisitions beyond the comprehension of common folk. He would have divided God into persons and qualities and aspects. Being the Son of God He simply spoke of Him as Father. His Father and our Father. He assumed God as we assume our fathers. He talked of Him not as a far-off Deity sitting on an embroidered divan, ruling suns and moons and stars, but as an ever-present Parent who was interested, not merely in nations, but in men and women and children. He lived in God's atmosphere. He practised God's presence. The God consciousness was evidenced in all He did and in all He said. His programme was to transmit God consciousness to others —not by the process of fear, but by love. The fear element obscures God. Love enables us to understand Him. Only by the domination of love over fear can we see things as the Father sees, and think as the Father thinks. Just in proportion as we substitute a theologian for Jesus or a theology for religion we get fear. Men despaired of an intimate association with Deity. Jesus persuades them that the Father is interested in the individual man. He tells them that God is not unconscious of the fate of a sparrow. If He cares for a sparrow He surely cares for a human being. That appeals to men. It gives them a new hope, a new point of view. He says, '**Even the hairs of your head are all numbered.**'

He was surrounded by the poor, the day labourers, and the social outcasts. They had a struggle to live

the physical life. He assures them that faith in the
Father assures them of food for the body and food
for the soul. His meaning is never hidden in words.
He is no mystic dealing in empty, pious phrases. Having
suffered, He knew how to sympathise with suffering;
having been tempted He understood the conflict between
the higher and the lower nature. Jesus sees in the Father
a heart so tender and loving that He makes the sun to
shine upon the unjust as well as upon the just. All are
His children. All are equally dear to Him. He drives
this home by the most charming stories of large-hearted
men. He shows how the strength of God is demonstrated
in helping weak men out of great difficulties. He paints
a word picture of the yearning heart of the Father as
He awaits the return of the soul that has strayed out
of the path. This dependence and interdependence—
this affinity of the divine and human, this nexus of God
and man, is the quintessence of the Gospel—the Good
News.

How can we acquire it? they asked. He told them.
He that receiveth Me, receiveth the Father. Interpretation of personal life may be done in two ways.
We may explain the life of others in the terms of our own
personal experience, or we may reproduce the life of
another in experiments of our own. Jesus was a perfect
translation of the will of the Father. When men saw
that, they were encouraged to make spiritual experiments
in their own lives. They accepted His view of Himself
and the Father. As they began to think His thoughts
their inner being changed into His likeness. As a flower
absorbs sunshine and moisture and reproduces them in
beauty and colour, so men's lives changed in essence and
outlook. The change was spiritual and subtle. It came
without observation. The alembic in which these
changes were wrought was prayer, and the process was
faith. Jesus used no theological or philosophical terms
in directing men's minds towards this change. He
simply practised the life and men seeing the life experimented with it, and the experiments became experience
and the experience became faith, and faith connected

them intimately in a bond of filial love with the Father.
It is in filial *experience* then that the Father is found.
The other half of the truth is, that in the discovery of
the Father, we discover also that all men are our brothers
and all women our sisters. It is a family consciousness,
an enlarged outlook. The thing that hurts and hinders
others will hurt and grieve us. What gives them joy
will gladden us. Cultivated and developed, this consciousness evolves in love, and love is the essence of the
life of the spirit. This otherism does not confine itself
to humans. It takes in the life of all created things,
animate and inanimate. In the tint of a sunset, the
contour of a mountain, the surge of the sea, the song of a
bird, and the colour of a flower, we see the Father's hand
and we rejoice in His handiwork. A filial, childlike
trust in the Father's plan; a simple experience of love
that responded to the beauty of the world and was solici-
tous of the claims of others' needs, was the open sesame
to the mystery of God. In this sense Jesus was the
Way. He was its revelation and its exemplification.
In the most exquisite poetic language He drew attention
to the beauty of the world and in personal touch with
men He exemplified God's solicitude and care for
human needs. To experience these things was to
know God, and to know Him is a vastly different
thing from knowing *about* Him. There is no way but
the way of experience, and no door but the door of
doing. **'If ye know these things, happy are ye if ye
do them.'** How shall we know? they asked, and He
told them they would know by the same method as
the man who found treasure in a field, and in joy went
and sold all that he had and bought the field. He told
also of a man who did the same thing in order to possess
a pearl of great price. The value of the thing discovered
gave joy, and joy was evidence. In their search for
the Father that was all the evidence they would need,
and as He had it, and they saw the evidence in Him,
they experimented upon themselves. They were all
different and would find different avenues of approach,
but all approaches led to the same goal. Some found

God in a dynamic way, others came to the knowledge in quietness and confidence. The joy of knowledge came more slowly to some than to others.

He told men to have faith in God—to assume Him as He did. He advised them to enter their quiet rooms and shut the door and there alone with God tell Him the story of their hearts in prayer—and prayer was a *pouring out* of a human heart to the heart of the divine. It was the act of relating needs to the source of supply. It was communion. There were times when perspiration rolled down the cheeks of Jesus when He was in the act of prayer, and the drops of sweat were likened to drops of blood. Sometimes He prayed all night. Often He prayed alone. In urging His disciples to pray, he said, '**Knock and it shall be opened unto you, seek and ye shall find.**' When their minds tire and their souls get weary and the result is doubt, He reminds them that any father will give his children what is good for them, and then asks them if they think the Heavenly Father has less heart—less affection? Things needful for the body were essential and the disciples and the people around them were being constantly reminded of their needs and of the relation between demand and supply. A man asked Him to arbitrate an economic question between him and his brother. Jesus refused. He said He was not a divider of property and added:—

'Beware of covetousness, for a man's life does not consist of the things that he possesseth.'

Then He told the story of the rich fool who accumulated goods and starved his soul. Using the story as a contrast between the needs of the body and the needs of the soul He spoke of God's care for the ravens and the lilies and the grass. '**O little faithed ones,**' He said, '**your Father knoweth what ye are in need of.**' Then He explains the first step—not in the economic process but in spiritual progress The nations of the world emphasise economics. That is necessary, but in the Kingdom first things are first.

'Seek ye the kingdom, and all these things will be added unto you.'
It is a matter of emphasis. The labour of the hands would still be necessary to procure food, but food for the soul was more necessary and the adoption of the Kingdom was the point of departure to the eternal journey of the soul. It was the Way to God, and He Himself was the door. To enter was the beginning of God-consciousness. It was to think His thoughts and do His work. To those who wanted to locate the Kingdom He said it was within them. To another who wanted to locate the Father, He said:—
'God is Spirit.'
The Samaritans located on Mount Gerizim the special earthly abode of God. To the Jews it was in Jerusalem. To Jesus it was neither and both. Spirit can *not* have a local habitation. Being Spirit it becomes necessary to worship Him only in spirit and in truth.

¶ 153

The Father's Love

For the mind of the beginners Jesus drew a series of word pictures of the Father. The best of them is the father of the prodigal. His father-heart never ceased to mourn the absence of the son. The boy's return finds him as he left him—loving, tender, and true. The father-heart is full of joy and overflows into merry-making. This, Jesus says, is what happens in heaven when the Kingdom enters your heart and reveals the Father. He likens Him to a man who forgives those who owe him money, and in the pattern prayer he taught the disciples to ask the Father to cancel their debts They were to cancel the debts of others and to give and lend and ask nothing in return Thus to share in the work of the Father was to glorify Him. When Rome and the hierarchy should arrest and arraign them they were not to worry over the form of words used in their defence.

'The spirit of your Father which is within you will speak.'

In this way He identified the spirit of man with the spirit of the Father. The Spirit speaking in them was another evidence of unity.

'If ye know me ye know the Father also.'

was another self-evident truth that their minds comprehended and their eyes beheld. Looking out into the future, He saw them lose some of that unity, and He prayed that they might be one—one in purpose as were the Father and Son.

The records are fragmentary. There is little recorded about God's intimate relation to the great world around them. When He speaks of God caring for birds and flowers and grass we have a suggestion of much that is not recorded at all. The suggestion is enough. The Kingdom did not furnish text-books on science. It was purely a philosophy of the soul and the soul's relations, and the chief relationship was the relationship of men and women and children to the Father.

At the heart of the Kingdom was the King, and the King was God, and God was a loving, forgiving, generous over-Parent, whose chief concern was His subjects, and His subjects and citizens were the pure in heart, the ready of hand, and the sincere seekers after truth. God, as Jesus described Him, was an atmosphere in which the soul found health and healing and strength. It was all so plain, so understandable, and so human-like.

On the eve of His great crisis He spoke of the cup which the Father had given Him—the cup of sacrifice, but the cup of joy came from the same Fatherly hand. He lived and moved in the Father's presence. He was at one with Him in life and purpose. He changed the abode of God from a corner in the Temple out into the open world—out into every home, every heart, every city and village, every mountain and meadow. Wherever the heart of man grew weary or suffered pain, there was the Father. Not any longer the awful Deity of the Jews merely, but the Father of the human race!

Lightning Source UK Ltd.
Milton Keynes UK
UKHW020635060223
416537UK00012B/2633